PROCEEDINGS OF THE
TWELFTH INTERNATIONAL CONGRESS
OF THE
INTERNATIONAL ORGANIZATION
FOR MASORETIC STUDIES

1995

# THE SOCIETY OF BIBLICAL LITERATURE
## MASORETIC STUDIES

Edited by
E.J. Revell

Number 8
PROCEEDINGS OF THE
TWELFTH INTERNATIONAL CONGRESS
OF THE
INTERNATIONAL ORGANIZATION
FOR MASORETIC STUDIES

1995

Edited by
E.J. Revell

PROCEEDINGS OF THE
TWELFTH INTERNATIONAL CONGRESS
OF THE
INTERNATIONAL ORGANIZATION
FOR MASORETIC STUDIES

1995

Edited by
E.J. Revell

Published by
SCHOLARS PRESS
for
The Society of Biblical Literature
and
The International Organization for Masoretic Studies

# PROCEEDINGS OF THE TWELFTH INTERNATIONAL CONGRESS OF THE INTERNATIONAL ORGANIZATION FOR MASORETIC STUDIES

## 1995

edited by
E. J. Revell

**Library of Congress Cataloging in Publication Data**
International Organization for Masoretic Studies. International
   Congress (12th : 1995 : Cambridge University)
     Proceedings of the twelfth International Congress of the
   International Organization for Masoretic Studies, 1995 / edited by
   E.J. Revell.
       p.   cm. — (Masoretic studies ; no. 8)
     Includes bibliographical references and index.
     ISBN 0-7885-0180-1 (cloth : alk. paper)
     1. Masorah—Congresses. 2. Bible. O.T.—Criticism, Textual—
   Congresses. I. Revell, E. J. (Ernest John), 1934–  . II. Title.
   III. Series.
   BS718.I57   1995
   221.4'4—dc20                     96-26262
                                        CIP

   ISBN 978-1-58983-487-3 (paperback : alk. paper)

Printed in the United States of America
on acid-free paper

# TABLE OF CONTENTS

v

vi

# PREFACE

The majority of the papers printed in this volume were presented at the Twelfth International Congress of the International Organization for Masoretic Studies, held at Cambridge on the sixteenth of July, 1995. Two papers presented at that congress have not been included. Maria Josefa de Azcárraga spoke on "An Analytical Index of the Masora of the Cairo Codex", giving a description of the ongoing programme of work which she did not wish to publish in that form. Geoffrey Khan read a paper on "The Pronunciation of *Resh* in the Tiberian Reading Tradition" which he had arranged to publish in the *Hebrew Union College Annual*. The volume also includes papers read at other meetings in the United States by Richard Goerwitz, Saul Levin, and Abraham A. Lieberman.

The majority of the papers were printed using "Nota Bene" as the word processor, a programme admirably suited to work of this kind. Some contributors had to go to considerable trouble to transfer their text from their own programmes into a form accessible to Nota Bene. I am most grateful to them for this, and to my colleagues here, in particular Prof. J. S. Holladay, who responded readily whenever I had to call for technical assistance. Despite its general excellence, Nota Bene is not equipped to answer every specialist need. Some contributors have had to accept a less precise use of symbols than they would have liked. I am grateful for their forbearance. Others, for similar reasons, or because transfer from thrie own programmes was simply impossible, produced their own camera-ready copy. I am grateful to them for their careful work, and their patient response to my requests for changes to bring their copy closer in form to that produced in Toronto. As usual, the excellent organization of Scholars Press made the process of production easy, and questions regarding it were quickly and helpfully answered by the Associate Director in charge of publications, Dennis Ford. I am most grateful to him for his help.

The Cambridge Congress took place in association with the Fifteenth Congress of the International Organization for the Study of the Old Testament (July 16 -21, 1995). As usual, the help and hospitality of the larger organization made the association a pleasure. We owe particular thanks to Dr. G. I. Davies, the Secretary of the I.O.S.O.T Congress, for his help with organization and registration, and for arranging for us the pleasant room in St. John's College in which to meet.

The meeting began with opening remarks from our President, Prof. Aron Dotan. Among the various I.O.M.S. matters he dealt with, he extended thanks to our Secretary-treasurer, Rabbi Milton Weinberg, for his part in the organization of the meeting. The success of this and other meetings of the I.O.M.S. is due in large part to the unflagging zeal of Rabbi Weinberg's work on behalf of the organization. When the Cambridge meeting was over, he was soon busy with arrangements for future meetings in New Orleans in 1996, in Jerusalem in 1997, and possibly in Oslo in 1998. The I.O.M.S. owes a great deal to Rabbi Weinberg's activities as Secretary, and it is pleasant to have an opportunity to recognize this, and to offer our thanks to him.

# MASORETIC SCHOOLS IN THE LIGHT OF SAADIA'S TEACHING

Aron Dotan

Tel-Aviv University

Aaron Ben-Asher's renown as a leading masorete and authority is unquestionable and has been an undisputed convention for many generations. However, regarding the beginning of this reputation we are still in the dark. During the recent years of increasing interest in the study of Ben-Asher's Bible Masora, two trends of thought become prominent.

According to one, which seems natural and evident at first sight, Ben-Asher was regarded as a great scholar already in his lifetime. His learning and erudition, and perhaps also the fact that he descended from a prestigious dynasty of ancestors learned in Masora, made him an outstanding master masorete, already in his lifetime. His codices were being copied as master texts in his time and in generations to come, and it was only natural for Maimonides, two centuries later, to set his codex as model and adopt his readings as exemplary and *halakhically* binding. As a result, Ben-Asher's name became even more famous and spread all over the *halakha*-abiding Jewish world.

Another approach has it that in his time Aaron Ben-Asher was yet one of a group of masoretic scholars in Tiberias, constituting part of the Tiberian school of Masora. His descent from a family of masoretes may have given him some advantage over other scribes, and he was perhaps approached more often than others for his masoretic teaching,

1

and thus had perhaps more occasion to imprint his seal on biblical codices. After his death, when it turned out that he was the last of the Ben-Asher family of masoretes, his codices gained in standing and in prestige, which grew gradually even more in the course of the generations. But it was Maimonides who selected Ben-Asher's codex as master-codex, and by endorsing his readings *halakhikally*, gave him promotion to the highest grade as the master masorete, bestowing on his readings a certain normative status. Only since Maimonides, and only thanks to him, did Ben-Asher attain the binding authority which he has held ever since.[1]

The argument cannot be settled by speculation. No theoretical consideration could decide the issue either way. Each one of the two approaches is possible and coincides with some of the historical data. The issue can be settled only by first-hand contemporary evidence. Such evidence is very scarce, and until now almost non-existent. We may perhaps find some help in the grammatical writings of Rav Saadia Gaon.

Before going into the details of the evidence, let us first establish the chronological connection. It is commonly known that Saadia and Aaron Ben-Asher flourished at about the same time, namely at the end of the ninth and the beginning of the tenth centuries. For Saadia we have the exact dates - born 882, died 942. For Aaron Ben-Asher, instead of his exact dates, we have the date of his father's Moses Codex - 895, which places the son Aaron in the same generation as Saadia.

---

1. Both approaches were discussed by M. H. Goshen-Gottstein, "The Rise of the Tiberian Bible Text", *Studies and Texts*: Vol. I, *Biblical and Other Studies*, edit. A. Altmann (Harvard 1963), p. 117-121. He tends basically towards the first approach.

Moreover, it seems quite clear that their proximity goes even beyond chronology. In his wanderings from Egypt, where he was born, to Iraq where he ended his life, Saadia lived for many years in Palestine as well. He must have lingered for some years in Tiberias, in those days a centre of learning and literature, where masoretes and poets glorified the city with their works. Chronological analysis of the evidence concerning Saadia's whereabouts gives rise to the assumption that he stayed in Tiberias between 915 and 921. During those years, he came close to the local sages and was influenced by them, at least inasmuch as his own literary activity was concerned. As I have been able to show in the introduction to my forthcoming edition of Saadia's Grammar,[2] it was in those years that he wrote the first draft of his Grammar, and perhaps also some of his liturgy.

Consequently, the masoretic information which can be gleaned from his Grammar can teach us about his connections to the Masora and about masoretic conventions current in that community.

In the paper I read at our previous IOMS Congress in Jerusalem,[3] I have shown Saadia's close connection to Masora and masoretic sources, and how he managed to use this material as building stones in his Grammar.

This time we I try to look into his masoretic material from another point of view in order to learn from him something about the two master masoretes, Ben-Asher (henceforth: BA) and Ben-Naphtali (henceforth: BN), and the impact of their teachings during their lifetime.

---

2. כתאב פציח לגה אלעבראניין - in process of publication in the series "Sources for the Study of Jewish Culture" of the World Union of Jewish Studies.

3. "שקיעי מסורה בדקדוקו של רב סעדיה גאון" (=Vestiges of Masora in Saadia Gaon's Grammar), *Proceedings of the Eleventh Congress of the International Organization for Masoretic Studies (IOMS)*, Jerusalem 1994, p. 7* - 16*.

One must not expect to find the names of these scholars in Saadia's writings. Saadia did not make a habit of mentioning other people by name. However, close scrutiny of some of the readings he propounds reveals his attitude.

A clear affinity with BN can be traced in Saadia's rules about the *dagesh lene*. As is well-known, this *dagesh*, which is due in the letters בגדכפ"ת at the beginning of words, fails if the previous accentually-connected word ends with a vowel.[4] This rule has several exceptions, enumerated in detail by Saadia. The exceptions, too, are formulated by general rules. In addition to these rules of exception, some ten isolated words carry the *dagesh* exceptionally without any rule. The exact number and nature of these exceptional words vary in different sources, and the details constitute a cause for controversy between BA and BN.

According to Mishael Ben ʿUzziel in his *Kitāb al-Ḫulaf*,[5] BN points a *dagesh* in s e v e n words following וַיְהִי , where the *dagesh* is not permitted by the rule and according to BA. These are the words:

| | |
|---|---|
| (Esth. 5:2) | וַיְהִי כִּרְאוֹת הַמֶּלֶךְ |
| (Jud. 11:35) | וַיְהִי כִרְאוֹתוֹ אוֹתָהּ |
| (Jos. 9:1) | וַיְהִי כִּשְׁמֹעַ כָּל הַמְּלָכִים |
| (Gen. 39:15) | וַיְהִי כְשָׁמְעוֹ כִּי הֲרִימוֹתִי |
| (Deut. 2:16) | וַיְהִי כַּאֲשֶׁר תַּמּוּ כָל אַנְשֵׁי |
| (Gen. 19:17) | וַיְהִי כְהוֹצִיאָם אוֹתָם הַחוּצָה |
| (1 Kings 15:29) | וַיְהִי כְמָלְכוֹ הִכָּה אֶת כָּל |

---

4. This rule of Saadia was discussed in the paper mentioned in the previous note, p. 12* - 16*.

5. *Mishael Ben Uzziel's Treatise on the Differences between Ben Asher and Ben Naphtali*, edit. L. Lipschütz, Jerusalem 1962 [=*Textus* 2 (1962), Supplement].

They take the *dagesh* exceptionally, contrary to the rule, according to BN.

In his Grammar, in the chapter on *dagesh* and *rafe*, Saadia enumerated the ten common exceptional words: מי כמכה (Ex. 15:11), גאה גאה (x2: Ex. 15:1,21), ידמו כאבן (Ex. 15:16), ושמתי כדכד (Is. 54:12), נלאיתי כלכל (Jer. 20:9), גדבריא דתבריא (x2: Dan. 3:2,3). To these he added "all ויהי כשמעו, ויהי כשמע",[6] two of the seven exceptional words of BN that have *dagesh*. In the revised version of this chapter on *dagesh* and *rafe*,[7] Saadia repeats only "all ויהי כשמע", and this is his formulation also in his commentary to Sefer Yeṣira.[8]

Moreover, *Kitāb al-Ḥulaf* shows us that while BA adds to the ten exceptions also עם זו גאלת (Ex.15:13) with *dagesh*, BN points it *rafe* according to the rule. Saadia does not list this word among the exceptions, thus implying a ruling like BN.

In his list of exceptions, Saadia brings both words גדבריא דתבריא (Dan. 3:2,3) as pointed b o t h with *dagesh* exceptionally. Again this is BN's reading in *Kitāb al-Ḥulaf*, whereas BA has an exceptional *dagesh* only in דתבריא, while גדבריא is *rafe*.

In another case, not related to *dagesh*, Saadia's reading goes against an agreement between both masters: in Jud. 21:19 he reads לַמְסִלָּה, whereas they both agreed לִמְסִלָּה. On the other hand, we find him in agreement with them both when he instructs the reader that the *resh* of נִירְשָׁה (Ps. 83:13) is (pronounced) with *patah*, namely its *shewa* is

---

6. ויהי כשמע occurs seventeen times in all. The reading of ויהי כשמעו (Gen. 39:15) in the manuscript is somewhat doubtful, but we assume it is correct.

7. Two editions of the chapter on *dagesh* and *rafe* by Saadia himself came down to us, both will appear in my edition mentioned above ( see note 2).

8. ספר יצירה [כתאב אלמבאדי] עם פירוש הגאון רבנו סעדיה ב"ר יוסף פיומי, edit. J. Kāfiḥ, Jerusalem 1972, p. עט.

mobile, just as Mishael quotes בפתחה נְבֶשָׁה as an agreement between BA and BN. So far regarding readings attributed expressly to the great masters.

However, Saadia's readings can also be compared to BA by implication, namely, in comparing Saadia's readings to Bible codices attributed to BA or his school.

For instance, Saadia teaches us along with his rules on the *shewa* that the *shewa* of *zayin* in יְשֵׁיזְבְכוֹן (Dan. 3:15) is quiescent (נח), whereas the *shewa* of *zayin* in יְשֵׁיזְבִנָּךְ (Dan. 6:17) is mobile (נע). The evidence of the Leningrad Codex B19a (henceforth: L) is to the contrary: it has יְשֵׁיזְבְכוֹן with a *ga*$^c$*ya* under *shin*, indicating that the following *shewa* is mobile. As opposed to that, the lack of a *ga*$^c$*ya* in יְשֵׁיזְבִנָּךְ may point to a non-mobile *shewa*. L is an accepted source for BA readings (in the Aleppo Codex [henceforth: A] this part is missing), and in this detail, this must have become the accepted reading, since out of the huge bulk of manuscripts compared by Ginsburg,[9] four are found with *ḥatef pataḥ* in יְשֵׁיֲזְבְכוֹן, namely a *shewa* mobile, but none at all in יְשֵׁיזְבִנָּךְ. Consequently, we may conclude that Saadia, in differing from all these sources, differs essentially from BA. We do not have BN's reading in these words.

For the sake of the evenness of the picture we should mention two words where Saadia's reading agrees with the BA codices, namely אַשְׂבִּיעֶךָ (Ps. 81:17), as found also in A and L (as opposed to the common אַשְׂבִּיעֶךָ), and the exceptional pointing וּמְרָגְזֶךָ (Is. 14:3) found also in A (although L has וּמֵרָגְזֶךָ). Since we do not have BN's reading, we do not know whether in these two items there was a disagreement between the two masters, so that Saadia's agreement with BA codices would mean nothing.

---

9. *The Writings*, edit. C. D. Ginsburg, London 1926.

Coming now to evaluate these findings, we can state with certainty that

a) none of Saadia's quoted readings coincides with BA against BN,

b) most of the readings which could be placed are BN's, and

c) Saadia may (in one or more cases) be in disagreement with both masoretes.

How do these points permit us to place Saadia among the Tiberian masoretes, specifically between BA and BN ?

The evident discrepancy between Saadia and BA must be considered and can be interpreted in different ways. We suggest the following solution.

One may argue, on the basis of point (a) that BA at that time had not yet become a generally accepted authority, at least not the kind of authority he grew to become in later generations.

It does not stand to reason that Saadia opposed BA's readings as a matter of principle, for then we might have heard about it.[10] It would seem rather that the clear-cut split between BA and BN did not yet

---

10. The old belief that Saadia was a bitter opponent of Aaron Ben-Asher and attacked him in his poem אשא משלי on account of his Karaism, proved to be unfounded, as has been shown already thirty years ago by the present author ("האמנם היה בן-אשר קראי?", סיני, כ [תשי"ז]), and by M. Zucker ("נגד מי כתב רב סעדיה גאון את הפיוט 'אשא משלי'", רפ-שיב, שנ-שסב [תשי"ז], תרביץ, כד [תשי"ח], 355-362), and again see my *Ben Asher's Creed - A Study of the History of the Controversy (Masoretic Studies,* 3 [1977]). Following these studies it is clear today that Ben-Asher was not a Karaite, and that the response אשא משלי was not directed at Aaron Ben-Asher. It was directed either at a member of another Ben-Asher family who indeed was a Karaite (thus Dotan), or against somebody else, the title attributing it to 'Ben-Asher' being an erroneous later addition and should be ignored (thus Zucker). Be it as it may, no evidence of a close connection between the two Tiberian sages is known, consequently there is no ground to assume preference of Biblical readings on the part of Saadia, neither adoption nor rejection on a personal level. We have no evidence that his choice was biased.

exist in those days. Saadia adopted readings according to his judgement. The fact that none of these was obviously of BA (but see further on) may be taken as sheer coincidence. All the more so, they can easily be understood as a coincidence since we are speaking all in all of three definite BN readings, or we should really say 'what was later to become official BN readings', because at that time the renown of both was not what it later grew to become.

On the other hand, Mishael's list of exceptional BN dagesh, of which only ויהי כשמע (and perhaps ויהי כשמעו too) is accepted by Saadia, still contains five (or six) cases not mentioned by Saadia, persumably because they were not acceptable to him, in other words, he preferred the BA reading in these cases.

Perhaps we should imagine that all kinds of readings were discussed in the circles of masoretes. Scribes would prefer this or that reading, according to their own discretion, without making themselves part of this or that group.

An example would be, for instance, the masorete Ephraim Ben Buyāᶜa, who vocalized the Pentateuch Codex written by his brother Solomon Ben Buyāᶜa, the scribe who allegedly wrote the Aleppo Codex too. This Codex (Leningrad, Firkovitch II, no. 17) was completed in the year 930. Ephraim Ben Buyāᶜa was then a contemporary of Aaron Ben Asher, yet his readings are balanced between BA and BN, showing no preference for either of them and often deviating from both of them. Assumably he made his own choices. There was in his time no masoretic authority that had to be strictly obeyed.

This is what Saadia did too: he either followed his own judgement, or adhered to a certain masorete whose teaching he preferred *ad hoc*.

Out of this discussion and the varying practices grew the famous schools. BA and BN, too, made their choices. They did not invent new readings. They selected for "their Masora",[11] for the codices which they prepared or checked, certain readings, which sometimes were no better than others, but which found priority in t h e i r eyes. Later, when they gained prestige and authority on personal grounds, their readings as well came to be regarded as authoritative, and therefore preferable.

We can say that, in this way, a process of masoretic codification took place, a codification that, as we assume, grew gradually during the years, and which finally received its *halakhic* imprimatur by the authority of Maimonides. He chose to lay his weight on Ben-Asher strictly because of the reputation the latter had already gained before, as can be inferred from Maimonides' own wording[12] הספר הידוע (=the well-known codex), ועליו היו הכל סומכין לפי שהגיהו בן אשר (=and everybody would rely on it because Ben-Asher corrected it).

Saadia's stay in Tiberias preceded this process. Even if it started in Ben-Asher's lifetime, it may have gained momentum only after Saadia's departure, leaving no trace on the minutiae of Saadia's Bible text.

---

11. Cf. Mishael Ben ᶜUzziel's formulation in reference to Ben-Asher (*Kitāb al-Ḥulaf* [above note 5], p. ד ): דכר פי מאסרתה (= he mentioned in h i s Masora).

רמב״ם, יד החזקה, הלכות ספר תורה, ח, ד .12

# MASORA OR GRAMMAR REVISITED

Emilia Fernández Tejero
CSIC. Madrid

The material and temporary boundaries, the frontiers between masoretic and grammatical methods, is a controversial subject that has been analysed from different angles: the masora is interested in simple numerical computations with no more aim than the register of a concrete spelling; or, the masora is in the origin of grammar, and some of its rules witness linguistic perceptions improper for mere guardians of the consonantal text.

A. Dotan, in an article indispensable for the subject, "מן המסורה אל הדקדוק", makes an exact distinction between the grammarian and the masorete:

המדקדק רואה את היער את היער כולו, המסרן מבקש את העצים היחידים.

He insists in the need of having extensive grammatical sense for dealing with exceptions; he defends the view that the pass from masora to grammar took place among the Hebrew scholars prior to Arab influence, and points out the existence among them of fine linguistic observations, similar to modern linguistic structural concepts.[1]

Part of this paper is an enlargement of the examples put forward by A. Dotan in his above-mentioned article. The texts I present have been taken from the masora magna of the Cairo codex. The content of the notes bends the balance sometimes against, sometimes in favor, of

---

1. *Lěšonénu* LIV (1990) 155-168.

the view that grammatical knowledge was impotant for the masoretes. I will put forward some examples I found out when preparing the alphabetical-analytical transcription of that masora.[2] The starting point of that transcription was our Alphabetical Index of the *masorot* of the codex,[3] in which we followed Mandelkern's alphabetical and grammatical order.[4] Nevertheless, when preparing the analytical transcription, I ocassionally had to break that order, and to join under the same heading words with different grammatical structure and even belonging to different roots, but sharing a similar masoretic information. In these cases the masoretes left aside grammar, being moved by mere homophonic or homographic reasons.

Let us see a few examples:

- תאכל shares the masoretic information in 2 Sam 22:9 and Isa 9:17 (third person feminine) and in 2 Kgs 7:19, Ezek 12:18 and 24:17 (second person masculine). The masora is only interested in the number of cases the word occurs.
- The same is the case with אספך, active participle with suffix second person singular in 2 Kgs 22:20, and first person singular masculine with suffix second person singular masculine in 1 Sam 15:6. The masora is interested in the *ḥaser* spelling.
- With הביא, infinitive construct *hifʿil* in Isa 1:13, Jer 17:24 and Ezek 20:15, and imperative *hifʿil* in Jer 17:18. The masora gathers the eight cases were the word occurs, with the note that seven of them have a *maleʾ* spelling (with a final א), and one has a *ḥaser* writing; this last

---

2. E. Fernández Tejero, *La masora magna del códice de Profetas de El Cairo*. Transcripción alfabético-analítica (Madrid: Consejo Superior de Investigaciones Científicas, 1995).

3. F. Pérez Castro, *El Códice de Profetas de El Cairo*. Edición de su texto y masoras dirigida por--- y realizada por C. Muñoz Abad, E. Fernández Tejero, M. T. Ortega Monasterio y M. J. Azcárraga Servert. Tomo VII: *Indice alfabético de sus masoras* (Madrid: Consejo Superior de Investigaciones Científicas, 1992).

4. *Veteris Testamenti Concordantiae Hebraicae atque Chaldaicae* (2 vols.; Graz: Akademische Druck- U. Verlagsanstalt, 1955).

case occurs in Ruth 3:15, as can be deduced from the *sîman*. This precision that appears in twelve of the sixteen lists checked by Ginsburg[5] led him to the conclusion that the masoretes took also this case as a *hifᶜil* form from the root בוא instead of from the root יהב, as is the analysis of Davidson,[6] and of Mandelkern.[7]

- With דברי, infinitive with suffix first person singular in Jer 31:20 and imperative singular feminine in Judg 5:12; numerical masora.

- With חגר, substantive in 2 Sam 20:8 and imperative in 2 Kgs 4:29; numerical masora.

- With הצא, third person singular masculine in Jer 51:10 and imperative singular masculine in Isa 43:8; the masora informs us that both cases are *roʾš pasûq*.

- With ויעלו, third person plural of the future *qal* in Joel 4:12 and *hifᶜil* in Ezek 27:30; numerical masora.

- With קנא, infinitive absolute *piᶜel* in 1 Kgs 19:10 and adjective in Josh 24:19. The masora is interested in the number and in the spelling.

- With ורבה, third person feminine of the perfect in Isa 6:12 and feminine adjective in Hos 9:7; numerical masora.

- With רעי in Isa 38:12, 44:28 and Zech 11:17, the morphological analysis is not clear. According to Davidson, in the first case it is an adjective, in the second a participle with suffix and in the third a substantive.[8] According to Mandelkern, the first one is a participle, the second a participle with suffix and the third a construct participle.[9] In any case, the masora is interested in the *ḥaser* spelling of the three passages.

- With תשיב, second person masculine of the future *hifᶜil* in Isa 36:9 and third person feminine in Judg 5:29; numerical masora.

---

5. *The Massorah Compiled from Manuscripts Alphabetically and Lexically Arranged*. With an Analytical Table of Contents and Lists of Identified Sources and Parallels by A. Dotan (4 vols.; New York: 1975) IV, 190.

6. *The Analytical Hebrew and Chaldee Lexicon* (London: Samuel Bagster & Sons, 1967), 162.

7. *Veteris Testamenti Concordantiae*, I, 464.

8. *The Analytical Hebrew Lexicon*, 687.

9. *Veteris Testamenti Concordantiae*, II, 1097.

- With משקה, construct participle in Hab 2:15 and construct substantive in 1 Kgs 10:21; numerical masora.

The masoretes even find it possible to mix different roots. Such is the case with ורעה, third person singular feminine *qal* of the root רעה in Jer 50:19, which shares the masoretic information with the feminine substantive of the root רעע in Jer 44:17. The masora is just interested in the number of times that the word occurs.

Nevertheless, the cases in which the masoretes inform us about grammatical differences, diverse roots or meanings referring to words that have a similar information, are as much or even more numerous. This is a point in favor of the practical value of their grammatical knowledge.

Let us see a few examples:

- מדין, prefix מ- with a substantive masculine singular of the root דין (Isa 10:2), shares the masoretic information with two other words spelled מדין, a proper noun in Josh 15:61, and a common noun masculine plural of the root מדד in Judg 5:10. In the case of Josh 15:61 the masora magna specifies:

מדין ג' וסימנהון במדבר (Josh 15:61), ישבי (Judg 5:10), להטות
(Isa 10:2). חד שם קרייה, וא' לש' דין וא' לש' לש' אורח.

In the masora magna of codex B19a there is no mention of the different meanings.[10] This is not the case either with list 101 in vol. II of Ginsburg, which has ג', בג' בג' לישני',[11] or with the masora magna of the Aleppo codex, which has the note ...ואינין בתלתה לשנין in Josh 15:61 and Isa 10:2. However, the information in both of these sources is more general than that of the Cairo codex.

Such are the data. If we adapted the order of the meanings --as it is offered by the masora of the Cairo codex-- to the biblical order, we would have the following identification: in Joshua a place name, in

---

10. G. E. Weil, *Massorah Gedolah iuxta codicem Leningradensem B 19a* (Romae: Pontificium Institutum Biblicum, 1971) list 1332.

11. *The Massorah*, II, 199, list 101.

Judges 'to judge', in Isaiah 'way'. But the problem would be: How to fit לש' אורח with the case of Isaiah?

Only in Judg 5:10 can a reference to אורח be found:

רכבי אתנות צחרות ישבי על מדין והלכי על דרך שיחו

but a root דין can also be adduced in this passage. The blame, nevertheless, must not be put on the masoretes. It would be enough to think that the identification of the *lišanîn* has not been given in the masora in the biblical order, a phenomenon we usually find. So the meaning 'to judge' would be ascribed to Isaiah, and 'way' to Judges.

The translation of מדין in this passage is problematic. According to Rashi, it has the meaning of 'to judge':

על מדין, לשון 'דיינים', שהיו יראים לעשות משפט בפרהסיא.א.12

For Radaq it is a place-name:

יושבי על מדין שיחו, והוא שם מקום הנזכר בספר יהושע... ואומר במסרה: "מדין ג' בג' לשני: מדין וסככה [שם]; יושבי על מדין; להטות מדין דלים [יש' י, ב] חד שם קרתא, וחד לשון 'אורח', וחד לשון 'דינ'".

The same is true for Ralbag:

רוכבי אתונות לבנות, שהיו יושבים על דרך מדין ומתעכבים שם, ולא יוכלו להשלים דרכם הישר מפני פחד אויב, ויטו דרכם ללכת על דרך אחר, והוא דרך שיחו.

Also for Yosef Qaro:

על מדין שם מקום הוא בארץ יהודה ושמו 'מדין', כדכתיב בספר יהושע.

However, we retrieve the meaning of 'to judge' in Isaiah di Trani:

והולכי על הדרך ממקום למקום לשפוט את ישראל... והם"ם של 'מדין' בא נוסף, כי דרך הם"ם להיות נוסף בשמות.

Modern criticism is also uncertain about the identity of the word. *The International Critical Commentary* qualifies the word as "noun... unknown", and remarks that

---

12. For the rabbinic commentaries, see M. Cohen, *Mikraʾot Gedolot 'Haketer'. Joshua-Judges*. Edited with an Introduction by --- (Jerusalem: Bar-Ilan, 1992) 108-109.

The older interpreters, by an impossible etymology, explain
it, *judgement*, or *place of judgement*; most moderns derive it
from מד... with Aramaic plural ending.
It proposes translating the term as
cloths; hence either, *saddle-cloths*, *housings*, or (rich) *carpets* (so the most).[13]
The *Interpreter's Bible* proposes 'carpets', and qualifies the word מדין
as unintelligible.[14] A. S. Hartom (in Cassuto's *Sifré ha-Miqra*) points
out the existence of two possibilities:

יש מפרשים מדין מלשון דין ולפי זה יושבי, כלומר יושבים, על
הדין, הם הדינים היושבים למשפט. אחרים סוברים כי מדין [= מדים]
הוא צורת רבים של השם מד, בגד מפאר, או שטיח, מרבד.[15]

Nevertheless, R. G. Boling's more recent commentary (*The Anchor
Bible*) defends the reading 'the judgment seat', and thanks Freedman
for his proposal of recognizing
the problematic *mdyn* in our verse as a noun with the typical
*mem* preformative derived from the verb *dyn*, "to judge".[16]

I have commented this passage in detail because in two prestigious
translations of the Spanish 16th century (both made from the original
Hebrew), the meanings proposed by the Jewish commentators are
kept.[17] The view that the word is a place-name is represented in the

13. G. F. Moore, *A Critical and Exegetical Commentary on Judges*. (Edin-
burgh: T. & T. Clark, 1949⁶) 148.

14. J. Bright and J. R. Sizoo, *The Book of Joshua* (New York: Abingdon
Press, 1953) 722.

15. מ. ד. קאסוטו, ספרי המקרא. ספר שפטים מפרש על ידי א. ש. הרטום. תל-
אביב 1962.

16. *The Anchor Bible. Judges*. Introduction, Translation and Commentary
by --- (New York: Doubleday & Company, 1981) 102 and 110.

17. Concerning the translation process of the most significant Spanish
Bibles, see N. Fernández Marcos, "La Biblia de Ferrara y sus efectos en las
traducciones bíblicas al español", in J. M. Hassán (ed.) con la colaboración de A.
Berenguer Amador, *Introducción a la Biblia de Ferrara* (Madrid: Consejo Superior
de Investigaciones Científicas *et al.*, 1994) 445-472.

Ferrara edition (1553), a very literal translation from Hebrew, as its authors, Yom Tob Atias and Abraham Usque, established in their *Prologo* ("Traduzida del Hebreo palabra por palabra"). The text reads:

Caualgantes asnas blancas estantes cerca Middin y andantes sobre carrera fablad,[18]

following the line of Radaq, Ralbag and Yosef Qaro. The meaning 'to judge' is suggested in the translation of Casiodoro de Reina (the so-called *Bear's Bible* because of its *ex libris*: a bear leaning on a tree and licking a honeycomb) where we find:

Los que caualgays en asnas blancas los que presidis en juycio, y los que ys camino, Hablad,[19]

following the line of Rashi and Isaiah di Trani.

Those traditions are lost in the contemporary translations into Spanish. F. Cantera translates:

Los que cabalgáis asnas blancas, los que os sentáis sobre tapices y quienes por la ruta camináis: ¡cantad![20]

L. Alonso Schökel translates:

Los que cabalgáis borricas pardas, sentados sobre albardas, de camino, atended.[21]

To sum up: it can never be stressed enough how much translators can benefit from the analysis of the masoretic notes and the interpretations of the Jewish commentators, even if they eventually reject them, as I already pointed out some years ago.[22]

---

18. Facsimile edition (Madrid: Consejo Superior de Investigaciones Científicas *et al.*, 1992) 114.

19. *La Biblia, qve es, los sacros libros del vieio y nvevo testamento.* (Basle: Guarin/Biener, 1569) 454.

20. F. Cantera Burgos y M. Iglesias González, *Sagrada Biblia.* (Madrid: Biblioteca de Autores Cristiano, 1975) 225.

21. L. Alonso Schökel y J. Mateos, *Nueva Biblia española* (Madrid: Ediciones Cristiandad, 1977²) 346.

22. E. Fernández Tejero, "Masora y Exégesis", in N. Fernández Marcos, J. Trebolle Barrera, J. Fernández Vallina (eds.), *Simposio bíblico español (Salamanca 1982)* (Madrid: Universidad Complutense, 1984) 183-192.

Let us run through some other examples:

- in יתרה, a common noun in Isa 15:7, and in יתרא, a proper noun in 2 Sam 17:25, the masoretic notes inform about the different spellings. They specify them as a kind of *caveat* against the homophony.

- נאכל, first person plural, future *qal* of the root אכל appears in Isa 4:1; נוכל, participle singular masculine of the root נכל appears in Mal 1:14; in both *masorot* the different spellings are specified and in the second passage the two roots are indicated.

- למד is infinitive absolute of the root למד in Jer 12:16 and infinitive construct of the root מדד in Zech 2:6; the *masorot* of the two passages specify that in the case of Zechariah the meaning is related to, so to speak, 'topography',[23] and, in the case of Jeremiah, to 'learning'.[24]

- יסערו in Hab 3:14 shares the masoretic information with ישערו in Ezek 32:10 (the note to this passage is found in an ornamental masora in Ezek 32:2); the spellings with ס and ש are specified.

- ותפוח is a common noun in Joel 1:12 and a proper name in Josh 17:8; the masora magna of both passages informs us about the semantic fields of the three passages involved: a place-name in Joshua,[25] a proper name in Cronicles,[26] and a tree name in Joel.[27]

---

23. ואֹ' לשון משיחה: "Then I asked, 'Where are you going?' He answered me, 'To measure Jerusalem, to see what is its width and what is its length'" (Zech 2:2. Translation from *The New Oxford Annotated Bible* [New York: Oxford University Press, 1989] 1222).

24. ואֹ' לשן יולפנ': "And then, if they will diligently learn the ways of my people, to swear by my name, 'As the LORD lives,' as they taught my people to swear by Baal, then they shall be built up in the midst of my people" (Jer 12:16, *The New Oxford Annotated Bible*, 982).

25. שם קריה: "The land of Tappuah belonged to Manasseh, but the town of Tappuah on the boundary of Manasseh belonged Ephraimites (Josh 17:8, *The New Oxford Annotated Bible*, 290).

26. שם ברנ': "The sons of Hebron: Korah, Tappuah, Rekem, and Shema" (1 Chr 2:43, *The New Oxford Annotated Bible*, 506).

27. לשון אילנין: "The vine withers, the fig tree droops. Pomegranate, palm, and apple, all the trees of the field are dried up; surely, joy withers away among the people (Joel 1:12, *The New Oxford Annotated Bible*, 1164).

A mere homophony, without homography, can also be in the base of a masoretic note:

- לכה in Isa 3:6 and ולכה in 2 Sam 18:22 are masculine pronouns second person singular; לך in Judg 19:13 is imperative of the root הלך. The note on the latter passage, under the masoretic heading לכה, enumerates the three cases of the root. Nevertheless, in the two first cases the rule concerning the pronoun is given, and afterwards the rule concerning the root הלך.

There are also cases of near-homophones where the masoretic information is not the same. So, in the note on ולרגלה, infinitive construct *pi'el*, the masora magna of 2 Sam 10:3 informs us that it is a *lêt* case, while in לרגלה in 1 Sam 25:42 the masora informs us about רגלה and לרגלה, without including, as happens in other notes, all the cases with a preformative. Since ולרגלה is a *lêt* case, it has received a different treatment.

The method can change: different cases of a form or of a root that share the masoretic information may be joined in a single masora. For example:

- The masora magna of Ezek 23:37, under the heading בניהן לבניהן ובניהן, indicates the *sîmanîm* of the three cases of the masculine plural noun with suffix of third person feminine plural. All the three cases are *lêt*, as confirmed by the masora parva of the passage: ג' א' לבנ' וא' ובנ', and by the masora parva of Ezek 16:45: ל'.
- This is also the case with the masora magna of בגורל in Josh 14:2, where, under the heading גורל, the four cases of the word in construct state, namely with *patah*, are recorded. The masora parva of the passage confirms the information: ד' בלש', while the masora parva of Josh 18:11 says ב' (the note concerns גורל exclusively) with the *sîman* of Ps 125:3.

A higher grammatical sensitivity is shown in rules concerning words that can be constructed with different prepositions. For example:
- The masora magna of אמתך in Isa 38:18 records the *sîmanîm* of the two cases preceded by אל (Isa 38,18.19), a third one preceded by על (Ps 115:1) and a fourth one preceded by ועל (Ps 138:2).

- There are long lists of pairs of the same word preceded by different prepositions.[28]
- Other notes deal with the régime that governs particular roots: so, in the masora magna of לדבר אותך in 1 Kgs 22:24 we are informed of the construction of צוה with the *nota accusativi* את, of דבר with the homographic preposition, and its exceptions, that is to say, of the nine cases in which דבר is followed by the *nota accusativi*.
- Or in פקד אל in Jer 50:18, where the masora deals with the usual prepositional régime of the verb, which uses על, except for four exceptions constructed with אל. Such notes reflect linguistic concepts resembling the 'Phrasal Verbs' of modern linguists; the utility of the information which they provide is beyond doubt.

The *masorot* also make reference to accents. I do not mean generalizations as *milʿel/milraʿ*, or so-and-so cases בטעם; I refer to specific cases where the masora graphically shows the correct punctuation:
- In והיתה, Zeph 2:6, the heading of the masora magna is pointed and, after the *sîmanîm* of the three cases that must be pointed with *geršayim*, the note informs us that the same occurs throughout all the Pentateuch, except for one case (Num 27:11): והיתה with *qadmaʾ/ʾazlaʾ*.
- In 2 Kgs 15:16, the masora magna of ההרותיה gathers the *sîmanîm* of eight words punctuated with *maʿarikîn* (*mêrkaʾ/tiphḥaʾ*), and the *sîmanîm* are marked with the signs for the corresponding accents.

The masora is interested in exceptions, in minutiae, in small details.[29] This, precisely, is a fundamental difference from grammar, the aim of which is to make rules. However, the masoretes, in some way, also made rules and formulated norms.

---

28. Cf. for example masora magna of אל בנימין (Judg 21:6); על תרהקה (2 Kgs 19:9); על עני (Isa 66:2); על המשפט (Isa 28:6).

29. Dr. Gómez Aranda informed me that in the twenty-sixth Annual Conference of the Association for Jewish Studies (Boston, December 18-20 1994) Dr. Marcus read a paper under the suggestive title "Protecting the Minority: The Democratic Principle of the Masora".

Perhaps something else can be added. If we analyse, for instance, the forty masoretic notes registered in the first chapter of Malachi --of course, in the Cairo codex-- we find out that eleven of them refer to the spelling of the text (therefore, to its safeguard), five of them are related to grammatical matters, and all the rest of them, twenty-four, have a numerical character.

The question is: what was the usefulness of numerical notes of this kind? To what extent did they help *soferîm* and masoretes to make a *seyag la-Torah*? What was the profit of a note stating the number of times a word appeared in a book or a group of books, but not specifying even the most elementary information, such as the spelling of the word?

A. Dotan, in the first paragraph of his article "Masorah" describes the evolution of the semantic field undergone by the term *sofer*:

which in the beginning was a term for scholars of the Torah in general, in time became limited to those scholars who specialized in the written Torah and its exact transmission... some were transcribers... while others were teachers and instructors of school children... and the original meaning of the term became obscured through its connection with the act of counting.[30]

Perhaps the masoretic notes of numerical character had a pedagogic aim, useless for the masorete but indispensable for teaching and memorizing the biblical text.

In the light of this reflection one can not avoid thinking of the Hebrew column of the Complutensian Polyglott, a work of at least three prominent Hebrew scholars, Pablo Coronel, Alfonso de Alcalá and especially Alfonso de Zamora.[31] Because in this column, the didac-

---

30. *Encyclopaedia Judaica*, vol. 16 (Jerusalem: Keter Publishing House, 1971) 1405.

31. Cf. the *Anejo a la edición facsímile de la Biblia Políglota Complutense* (Valencia: Fundación Bíblica Española/Universidad Complutense de Madrid, 1987) especially A. Sáenz-Badillos, "Hebraístas y helenistas complutenses", 15-20, and E. Fernández Tejero, "El texto hebreo", 25-32.

tic character of which is evident (it can be remembered, for example, that the complex tiberian system of accents was reduced to *sôph pasûq, 'atnaḥ* and a kind of *pašṭa'* over the stressed syllable in paroxitonal words), each of the words is marked with a letter and, in the margin, under the same letter, the root of difficult words is shown (see illustration). We have here a combination of masora --by reason of the place where the note is written--, with grammar --because of the information offered.

I have analysed examples of two kinds of phenomena that illustrate the existence of at least two sorts of *masorot* in their historical accumulative process (besides the numerical notes, of pedagogical character). On the one hand, there are notes interested in the spelling and devoted to the safeguarding of the text. On the other hand, there are some very elaborate notes, in which, as A. Dotan pointed out, a special linguistic sensitivity is revealed. According to him, the masoretes did not enunciate grammatical technical terms, but they did approach formal linguistic rules, depriving the masora of its primitivism and inspiriting its body with the gentle breeze of grammar.[32]

---

32. "מן המסורה", 162:

שאף על פי שלא הגיעה לידי ביטוי מוחשי במונחים דקדוקיים מוכרים, עדיין הייתה מבעבעת מתחת לפני השטח וממתינה לכלים הבלשניים הפורמליים שיגאלו אותה מהיוליותה, ויפיחו בה רוח של דקדוק חי.

A page of the *Biblia Polyglotta Complutensia*

# THE CAIRO *GENIZOT*
# AND
# OTHER SOURCES OF THE SECOND FIRKOVICH COLLECTION
# IN ST. PETERSBURG

Tapani Harviainen
University of Helsinki

The manuscript collections which originate from the Near East constitute also an important source for Masoretic studies. The Firkovich Collections in the National Library of Russia in St. Petersburg consist of 15,000 to 17,000 items, viz. large complete codices, manuscripts and manuscript fragments of various sizes, and other antiquities. This huge amount of material written mostly in Hebrew and Arabic was acquired by the famous Karaim scholar *Abraham Firkovich* (1787-1874) during his travels on the shores of the Black Sea, Dagestan, Caucasia, and the Near East.[1]

---

1. On the collections and their collector, see K. B. Starkova, "Rukopisi kollekcij Firkovicha Gosudarstvennoj publichnoj biblioteki im. M. E. Saltykova-Shchedrina" (*Pis'mennye pamjatniki Vostoka*, Istoriko-filologicheskie issledovanija, Ezhegodnik 1970, Moskva 1974, pp. 165-192); *idem*, "Les manuscrits de la Collection Firkovič (*Revue des Études Juives* 134, [1975]:101-117); Viktor Lebedev, "Jidishe ksavjaden in der leningrader efentlekher bibliotek", *Sovetish hejmland* 11/1989, Moskve 1989, pp.154-158; V. L. Vihnovich & V. V. Lebedev, "Zagadka 15 000 drevnih rukopisej (K sporam vokrug samoj bol'shoj v mire kollekcii vostochnyh rukopisej, hranjashchihsja v Leningradskoj publichnoj biblioteke im. M. E. Saltykova-Shchedrina, i lichnosti ee sobiratelja -- karaimskogo uchenogo A. S. Firkovicha)" (*Materialy po arheologii, istorii i*

The First Firkovich Collection includes the well-known Codex Leningradensis (I Firk. B 19a) and a great number of other biblical manuscripts, as well as large parts of the central Jewish and Karaite literature.[2] This collection was sold by Firkovich to the Imperial Public Library in St. Petersburg during 1862-63, i.e. before his last visit to the Near East.

His Samaritan Collection consists of 1,350 manuscripts. This collection was purchased by the Russian Minister of Public Worship in 1870.[3] Together with the Samaritan collection, the so-called Second Firkovich Collection houses the acquisitions made by Firkovich during his last *grand tour* in the Near East in 1863-65. The Second Collection consists of more than 13,000 manuscripts; 2,000 of them are biblical

*etnografii Tavrii*, vyp. II, Tavrija, Simferopol' 1991, pp. 130-140), and Tapani Harviainen "Abraham Firkovitsh och hans samlingar i *Rossijskaja nacional'naja biblioteka* i S:t Petersburg" (*Nordisk judaistik* 14:1 [1993], pp. 79-83).

2. Concerning the biblical manuscripts, see A. Harkavy und H. L. Strack, *Catalog der hebräischen Bibelhandschriften der Kaiserlichen Öffentlichen Bibliothek in St. Petersburg*. Erster und zweiter Theil (St. Petersburg - Leipzig 1874).

3. Haseeb Shedadeh, "Diwwuaḥ rishoni 'al 'osep kitbe ha-yad ha-shomroniyyim be-Sanṭ-Petersburg" (*Proceedings of the Eleventh World Congress of Jewish Studies*, Division D, Volume I, The Hebrew Language, Jewish Languages, Jerusalem 1994, pp. 61-64). On earlier catalogues and other details, see *Samaritjanskie dokumenty Gosudarstvenoj publichnoj biblioteki imeni M. E. Saltykova-Shchedrina - Katalog* (composed by L. H. Vil'sker och V. V. Lebedev. Ministerstvo kultury RSFSR. Gosudarstvennaja ordena trudovogo krasnogo znameni Publichnaja biblioteka im. M. E. Saltykova-Shchedrina. Sankt-Peterburg 1992), and Tapani Harviainen & Haseeb Shedadeh, "How did Abraham Firkovich acquire the great collection of Samaritan manuscripts in Nablus in 1864?" (*Studia Orientalia* 73, Helsinki 1994, pp. 167-192. Reprinted in *A. B. - The Samaritan News - Alef Bet - Ḥadashot ha-shomroniyyim*, 633-636, Holon, 13.4. 1995, pp. 180-158, and reviewed in Hebrew, *idem*, p. 6), p. 169 and fn. 10.

texts, and some 7,000 manuscripts are written in Judaeo-Arabic.[4] The Second Collection was acquired by the Imperial Public Library two years after the death of its collector in 1876, and the sum of the acquisition, 50,000 roubles (approx. £500,000 today), also covered the personal archive of Abraham Firkovich.[5]

In this survey of the sources of the Second Firkovich Collection, I shall follow the temporal order of his tour. A description of his itinerary therefore may be useful at the start.

During his third and last visit to the Near East, the seventy-six year old Abraham Firkovich arrived at Jaffa on October 3, 1863, two days later reaching Jerusalem by camel caravan. From Jerusalem he travelled via Jaffa and Beirut to Aleppo and later visited ancient Antioch, Alexandretta, and Beirut. Dangerous roads, however, caused an expedition to Damascus to be cancelled. Firkovich returned from Syria to Jerusalem on December 22, 1863. In March of 1864 he met the famous traveller and book-collector Jacob Sappir. In the same month he visited the Temple Mount in Jerusalem several times and dealt with the Karaite commissioners from Hīt, Mesopotamia. In April, Firkovich, together with his grandson Samuel, stayed for a fortnight among the Samaritans in Nablus (Sikem). They travelled together to Egypt in the middle of May. After spending the summer in Jerusalem, Abraham Firkovich and his young wife Hannah returned to Egypt. On March 19, 1865 they returned by boat from Istanbul to Evpatoria in the Crimea. But where Firkovich spent almost five months before his

---

4. Two inventory lists of these manuscripts have been published: Viktor Lebedev, *Arabskie sochinenija v evrejski grafike. Katalog rukopisej* (Ministerstvo kultury RSFSR. Gosudarstvennaja ordena trudovogo krasnogo znameni Publichnaja biblioteka im. M. E. Saltykova-Shchedrina. Leningrad 1987) and Y. Y. Yanon's (P. B. Fenton) preliminary *Reshimat kitbe-yad ba-'arabit-yehudit be-Leningrad: reshima 'ara'it shel kitbe-yad ba-'arabit yehudit be-'ospe Pirqobiṣ* (Makon Ben-Ṣebi, Jerusalem 1991).

5. Vihnovich-Lebedev, 1991:135.

return is still in need of additional light; at the end of 1864, however, he may again have visited Damascus.[6] Our knowledge of Firkovich's travels is based mainly on the letters kept in his personal archive. The following survey also refers to these letters in St. Petersburg. The majority of the correspondence is written in Hebrew, while a few letters are in Karaim, the Turkic language of the East European Karaites.

In spite of important discoveries, Firkovich seems to have been dissatisfied with the results at the start of his tour in Jerusalem. In a report of his activities written in the third person he says:[7] "And who would have told to Abraham that he will ascend the heights of the Holy Land a second time and will search the concealed underground storehouses (מטמונים) and from the Abyss of oblivion he will bring up antiquities of the sages of Israel, those of the Karaites and Rabbanites, the great and small, in Jerusalem." After these words, in contrast, he continues with real enthusiam: "in the city of Sikem, however (אך כי), he will find a comprehensive treasure (אוצר בלום) of Samaritan antiquities."

Before his great success among the Samaritans in April, Firkovich visited a number of Syrian cities. He mentions having had success in Antioch and Alexandretta (Iskenderun), where "also there he found interesting objects (דברי חפץ)."[8] In Aleppo he ascended "the tower of

---

6. This preliminary description is based on the letters in the Personal Archive of Firkovich kept in the National Library of Russia in St. Petersburg (F. 946, Lichnyj arhiv A. S. Firkovicha), cf. V. V. Lebedev, "Novye dannye o sobiratel'skoj dejatel'nosti A. S. Firkovicha" (*Vostochnyj sbornik GPB*, vyp. 4. Ministerstvo kul'tury RSFSR. Gosudarstvennaja ordena trudovogo krasnogo znameni Publichnaja biblioteka imeni M. E. Saltykova-Shchedrina. Leningrad 1990, pp. 32-44, esp. pp. 35-41), and Harviainen- Shedadeh, 1994. The documents dealing with the last visit to Damascus are kept in the *Krymskij oblastnoj gosudarstvennyj arhiv*, F.241. Op.I. X.I. No. 1868 (Lebedev 1990, p. 41, fn. 68).

7. Personal Archive, No. 478 (1r, Friday, 15 Elul 5624 = 16.9.1864) and its copy, No. 607 (4v), a letter to Abraham b. Judah ha-Miṣri.

8. *Ibidem.*

Joab ben Zeruiah" where once had been a stone with the Hebrew text "I, Joab ben Zeruiah, came here to Aram Zobah and occupied this tower."[9] The stone had fallen down from the wall of the tower in an earthquake in 1822, however, and had disappeared. With help of the local administration Firkovich searched for the inscription but he did not find it. Instead, he was able to acquire thirty-one books, some Syrian coins, Ammonite idols, an *ewangelia* manuscript in Arabic and Syriac, etc. He also visited the Great Synagogue in Aleppo and was allowed to see the famous Aleppo Codex; he describes both of them carefully and offers a copy of the colophon of the Keter (the Aleppo Codex).[10] I hope to have an opportunity to deal with this report which he sent from Aleppo to the Karaite *hakham* Nahamu Babovich in another context.[11]

After his return to Jerusalem, Firkovich consulted with the emissaries of the Karaite community of Hīt in Mesopotamia.[12] Its members wished to move to Jerusalem, and Firkovich supported this attempt with great sums of money. Two reasons motivated this support: (1) he wanted to enlarge the Karaite congregation in Jerusalem, where the number of local Karaites was not sufficient for one *minyan*;[13] and, (2) as a recompense he requested the community to deliver all of its manu-

---

9. אני יואב בן צרויה באתי פה לארם צובה וכבשתי את המגדל הזה.

10. Letters No. 478 (1r, 15 Elul = 16.9.1864; also its copy, No. 607, 4v), a letter to Abraham b. Jehudah ha-Miṣri, and letters Nos. 605, 1r-10v (12 Kislev 5624 = Monday, November 23, 1863), 489 (Friday, 22 Kislev 5624 = 3.12.1863; in fact 22 Kislev was a Thursday, which means that a mistake occurs in the date) and 340 (cf. Lebedev, 1990:35-37) to the Karaite *hakham* Nahamu Babovich.

11. With the exception of Hebrew quotations, the letter 489 was written in Karaim.

12. Firkovich had sent from Aleppo a letter to the Karaites in Hīt (letter No. 605, 19r-v).

13. For this purpose Firkovich sent a letter to the Karaite community in Constantinople asking for political and financial support for the plan of settlement (letter No. 605, 18v-19r, Thursday, 16 Adar Sheni 624, i.e. March 24, 1864).

scripts to him. A number of the Arabic transcriptions of Hebrew texts kept in the Second Firkovich Collection were no doubt delivered by these "Hītites" to Firkovich.[14] At the same time (in March) in Jerusalem, Firkovich met with the famous Rabbanite traveller Jacob Sappir, whom he eulogizes in his letters.[15] From him Firkovich bought - at a high price - some manuscripts and books which Jacob had brought from Yemen. He enumerated these acquisitions in one of his letters to his son-in-law Gabriel.[16] In an earlier paper entitled "How did Abraham Firkovich acquire the great collection of Samaritan manuscripts in Nablus in 1864?", Dr. Haseeb Shehadeh and I examined the history of the Firkovich collection

---

14. This transaction has been clarified in my article "Abraham Firkovitsh, Karaites in Hīt, and the Provenance of Karaite Transcriptions of Biblical Hebrew Texts into Arabic Script" (*Folia Orientalia*, Vol. XXVIII, 1991, Studies in Memory of Andrzej Czapkiewicz (1), Wrocław - Warszawa - Kraków 1992, pp. 179-191); see also Harviainen-Shedadeh, 1994:175, fn. 30. For these transcriptions and their supposed provenance, see *idem*, "Karaite Arabic Transcriptions of Hebrew in the Saltykov-Shchedrin Public Library in St. Petersburg" *[Estudios Masoréticos (X Congreso de la IOMS). En memoria de Harry M. Orlinsky.* Editados por Emilia Fernández-Tejero y María Teresia Ortega Monasterio. Textos y estudios "Cardenal Cisneros" de la Biblia Políglota Matritense (TECC) 55. Instituto de Filología del CSIS, Madrid 1993, pp. 63-72], and pp. 36-38 in *idem*, "A Karaite Bible Transcription with Indiscriminate Counterparts of Tiberian *qameṣ* and *ḥolam* (Ms. Firkovitsh II, Arab.-evr. 1)", in *Proceedings of the Eleventh Congess of the International Organization for Masoretic Studies (IOMS), Jerusalem, June 21-22, 1993*, ed. Aron Dotan (Jerusalem: The World Union of Jewish Studies, 1994, pp. 33-40).

15. Letter No. 605, 15r (to Jacob Sappir, Wednesday, 1 Adar Sheni = March 9) and 21r-22r (to his son-in-law Gabriel Firkovich, Tuesday, 21 Adar Sheni 624, i.e. March 29, 1864).

16. Letter No. 605, 21v-22r (to Gabriel Firkovich, Tuesday, 21 Adar Sheni, i.e. March 29, 1864).

of the Samaritan manuscripts and antiquities from Nablus - Sikem.[17] We unraveled in that paper the complicated story of the *two genizas* of the Samaritans, of the Samaritan Jacob al-Shelabi, "who is engaged in stealing from their sanctuary", of the rôle of the Samaritan priests in the sale of the *genizot*, and of Firkovich's vow to donate a great sum of money towards the repair of the Samaritan synagogue in Nablus. The story is a splendid testimony of Firkovich's abilities to persuade owners of antiquities to sell to him in particular.

In May Abraham Firkovich travelled to Cairo with his grandson Samuel. In his report he writes:[18] "And there he found 'the hidden portion of law-givers' (ספונה מחוקקים חלקת)[19] in the *geniza* of the ancient synagogue which is in the possession of the Karaites, a treasure of various ancient Karaite and Rabbanite books, complete and defective ones, about which we can say only: 'we have neither seen nor heard'; among the names of both the books and the authors there are those of which we have never heard. In fact, there are very, very few which are complete, in contrast with the number which are defective. Nevertheless, all of them are very advantageous (מועילים) and they will cast much light on the literature (ליטערטור) of the Karaites -- may God protect and preserve them."

When Abraham Firkovich returned after three weeks on June 6 to his wife Hannah in Jerusalem, he left Samuel in Cairo to clear the *geniza* of the Karaite synagogue; it was very large, and Samuel had no other help besides two *shammashim* of the community.[20] On June 16

---

17. Harviainen-Shedadeh in *Studia Orientalia* 73, 1994. Starkova (1974:168 and fn. 13) mentions that Firkovich was interested in the Samaritan manuscripts in Nablus already during his second visit in Palestine during 1840-41, and for this purpose he had acquired a recommendation letter written in Arabic in 1840.

18. No. 478 (1v-2r, Friday, 15 Elul = 16.9.1864) and its copy No. 607 (6r), a letter to Abraham b. Judah ha-Miṣri.

19. Cf. ספון מחקק חלקת (Deut 33:21).

20. Letter No. 608, paragraph *beth* (to Gabriel Firkovich, three slightly different copies on the 8th, 10th, and 16th, of June, 1864).

Abraham wrote to his son-in-law Gabriel[21] that in twenty-one days he and his grandson had been able to take out only half of the material found in the *geniza*, the second half remaining inside. Among his findings he enumerates an extensive grammar book of Hebrew written in Arabic,[22] valuable poetic books, "names of sages in their treatises of which we have not heard earlier", a colophon in a 930 years old *Sefer Torah* from Nisibis, books in Arabic, *targumim*, commentaries and *Seder toledot ha-neśi'im*.

Abraham Firkovich returned in September to Egypt. On the 14th of October he had to write to Gabriel that, in contrast to his earlier calculations, "the work in the *geniza* will be prolonged one more month, at least."[23] These short notes indicate that the material kept in the *geniza* in the Karaite synagogue of Cairo was very extensive: its evacuation and treatment demanded of several men at least six months work.

Abraham Firkovich was not satisfied, however, with the discovery of only one *geniza* treasure in Cairo. He also visited the synagogue of Ezra the Scribe in Old Cairo, which as a rule is referred to as The Cairo Geniza. But, in spite of two extensive descriptions, his visit leaves a number of questions unanswered.

Quoted above is his statement: "The work in the *geniza* will be prolonged one more month, at least." The next paragraph in the same letter reads:[24] "After that -- under the aegis of the *ḥakham bashi*[25] (בחשות החכם באשי) -- I intend below the dust to uncover the *geniza* which is in the synagogue attributed to Ezra the Scribe. I have already

---

21. Letter 608 (paragraph *beth*) from Jerusalem on 11 Sivan (June 16, the third, prolonged, copy).

22. Unfortunately, the book was defective at its beginning and at its end; he hoped, however, to find the missing parts among the numerous fragments which needed to be put in order.

23. Letter No. 610, 1r (14.10.1864): מלאכה הגניזה תתארך עוד לפחות חדש ימים.

24. *Ibidem.*

25. The *ḥakham bashi* was the leader of the local Jews in Egypt.

opened it and I have seen that there is hope to find interesting objects also there. It was not my plan, but it happened by chance that 'Abdallah's[26] wife, when being ill, had made a vow to go there (i.e. the Ezra synagogue, TH) to thank the Lord for being cured from her illness. Her husband also fulfilled her vow and he took his house members and us along, and we went there at his expense and spent three days there and on the fourth day we returned therefrom. During these days a doctor made a cure for my hands, because I had pains in the sinews. And from clay and lime I cleansed the texts which were in that synagogue and I copied them in a book. Although I did not find the date of its construction, I found the name of its founder who had founded it in the days of caliphs, i.e. in the days of the Prince 'Anan."

After this introduction, Firkovich describes the wall texts, the Torah arks (היכלים as the Sephardis also call them), and the Torah scrolls. I shall return later to the end of this letter.

We can first note, however, another letter in which Firkovich informs Abraham b. Jehuda ha-Miṣri of his work in Cairo.[27] The beginning of this report quotes the earlier passage concerning 'the hidden portion of law-givers' in the Karaite *geniza*. Firkovich then goes on to tell of his trip "to the Old Cairo which is called Fustat" (למצרים הישנה הנקרא פוסטט של מצרים) and to the Ezra synagogue. The Rabbanite *hakham bashi* was with him, and under his aegis he opened and scrutinized the famous Torah Scroll of Ezra the Scribe "from its beginning till the end." To his disappointment, however, its date was no earlier than "perhaps from the beginning of the sixth millenium" (i.e. the 13th century, TH) and in it there was nothing new to be found (ולא מצא שום דבר חדש). Because "the shadows of evening lengthened"[28] and Firkovich had not descended the סוף הקבלה of the synagogue, he returned the next day to examine the wall texts and Torah arks. However, the characters of the texts were full of mud and

---

26. It is obvious that 'Abdallah was the Rabbanite *hakham bashi,* cf. the second report below, letters 478 and 607.

27. No. 478, 1v-2v (16.9.1864), and its copy, 607, 6r-7v.

28. Jer 6:4.

lime. So Abraham Firkovich, then 76 year old,[29] climbed "... on long ladders in order to investigate the inscriptions, to make his work which he had attempted to make during many years, and he washed <them> well with water and read the inscriptions easily."

‫...בסולם הארוך לחקור הרשימות לעשות מלאכתו אשר נסה‬

‫זה כמה שנים, וירחץ במים היטב ויקרא את הרשימות בנקל.‬

He copied all the texts in detail and paid special attention to the fact that the Divine Name was written three times as *yod-waw-yod*, according to the Karaite habit.[30] Firkovich concluded on the basis of certain Arabic names that the synagogue had been built in the time of the caliphs. Thus, it could never have been a synagogue of Ezra, and the stories concerning the seat of Jeremiah and Elijah had been propagated by the Rabbanites in order to increase the glory of the synagogue, when, after the Karaites, they took possession of it.

Returning to the first-mentioned report of the Ezra synagogue (written on the 14th of October),[31] after giving a short description of the wall texts, Firkovich jumps abruptly to describing the eagerness of the Rabbanite leaders to open their *genizot*. He writes: "When (scil. the Rabbanite, TH) *ḥakham bashi* (scil. in Cairo, TH) heard tidings of the marvelous objects which have been found by me in the *geniza* of our brethren the Karaites here, there was a fire of desire burning in him to open their *genizot* too. However, until now I have not gone to him and have not talked to him about this matter. And the *ḥakham bashi* Rabbi Nathan of Alexandria has sent his son Abraham to me with the request that I should send him the translation by R. Saadia Gaon of the whole book of the Psalms which I have found, and I fulfilled his wish and received his favour. And even he consents to open the *genizot* which are there. And if you, my friend (i.e. Gabriel Firkovich, TH), will

---

29. His birthday was the 19th of Elul 5547 (= 2.9.1787) which, in 1864, occurred on (Tuesday) the 20th of September; cf. letter No. 610, 1r, and Lebedev, 1990:43 fn. 77, on the basis of Firkovich's autobiographic essay composed by him on his 77th anniversary (Personal Archive, No. 77).

30. In other texts, the Name consists of three *yods*.

31. Letter No. 610, 1r.

come, you will be able to perform their opening, and concerning me, my heart is firm, trusting in the Lord,[32] that you will be able to find more and more precious objects than in other places to which one has to travel quite a lot in order to search for them. Egypt, namely, is a country of wisdoms from days immemorial; this is enough for the wise."

Unfortunately, I have no source at my disposal which can clarify what the family of Firkovich did in the Ezra synagogue between the date of this letter (the 14th of October, 1864) and March 1865 when Abraham Firkovich left the Near East for ever.[33] He probably succeeded in collecting his whole family around him in Cairo; thus, he had no need to write letters.

In conclusion, we may state that (1) the majority of the manuscripts in the Second Firkovich Collection originate obviously from the *geniza* of the Karaite synagogue in Cairo. The long period of six months needed for the work there testifies in favour of this assumption, and the great number of fragmentary texts in the Second Collection -- in contrast to the First one -- lends additional support to it.[34] (2) Abraham Firkovich spent much money to buy antiquities and manuscripts which were in the possession of other persons; the case of Jacob Sappir and his expensive Yemenite books is an example of this policy, which he followed in the Syrian cities and elsewhere. (3) Since the 1830's Abraham Firkovich was very aware of the importance of the *geniza*s.[35] Thus, we have good reason to believe that, in each place Firkovich visited, he tried to find and examine these "hidden treasures." He managed to acquire the contents of the *genizot* of the

---

32. Cf. Ps. 112:7.

33. "Song of Thanksgiving" composed by Abraham Firkovich on board the SS Tamangur, 19.3.1865 (Personal Archive, No. 241, 2).

34. Cf. Starkova, 1974:175. A list composed by Firkovich of 246 manuscripts found in the "Cairo *geniza*" is included in the Personal Archive, No. 160 (פנקס הקדמוניות של גניזת מצרים), while the Mss. II Firk. Evr.-arab. 161 and 162 include a list of 666, resp. 675 manuscripts.

35. Starkova, 1974:168 and 171.

Samaritans in Nablus and the Karaites in Cairo in their entirety, and this may also be the case of the manuscripts of Hīt. The *firman* granted by Sultan Abdül Aziz and good relations with the political authorities in the Near East gave additional weight to his efforts to acquire the texts kept in the *genizot*. (4) Firkovich had entered the *geniza* of the Ezra synagogue with the consent of the Rabbanite leader. He was, thus, on good terms with him as well as with the *ḥakham bashi* of Alexandria and was given several months to investigate their *genizot*. Knowing the character of Abraham Firkovich, i.e. his unquenchable enthusiasm and his splendid powers of persuasion as well as his economic and polical power, his ambition for acquiring the treasures of these Egyptian *geniza*s did not end in complete failure.

One might to the contrary raise the question why anything was left over in the Cairo Geniza for Jacob Sappir, Adler, Schechter and their colleagues after his visit.

Finally, in order to demonstrate that the documents concerning Firkovich's discoveries in Cairo are not without enigmatic passages, I offer one more quotation from him. Concerning a manuscript of *Sefer ha-Hokhma*, he says: "These are the six folios which I brought out of the dark places of the cave which is located in the graveyard of our brethren the Rabbanites in New Cairo, close to Egyptian Zoan".[36]

---

36. הנה אלה ששת העלים אשר הוצאתי ממחשכי המערה אשר בבית החיים לאחינו הרבנים אשר במצרים החדשה הסמוכה לצען מצרים; Zoan of Egypt refers to Fustat. Firkovich's note in Ms. II Firk. Evr. II A, No. 190-8, quoted in L. H. Vil'sker, "Neizvestnye *mešālīm meḥōrāzīm* (rifmovannye pritchi) ili *"Sēfer ha-hoḥmā"* (kniga mudrosti) Sa'ida ben Babshada v Gosudarstvennoj publichnoj biblioteke im. M. E. Saltykova-Shchedrina v Leningrade" (*Occident and Orient. A Tribute to the Memory of A. Scheiber.* Budapest-Leiden, 1988, pp. 391-419), p. 391. I am grateful to Dr. Geoffrey Khan, who suggested that the note probably refers to the al-Basatin graveyard in Cairo.

# JEDIDIAH SOLOMON NORZI AND THE STABILIZATION OF THE TEXTUS RECEPTUS

Abraham A. Lieberman
Yeshiva University

J.S. Norzi (Minḥat Shai),[1] the great Masoretic scholar, played a very important role in the process of the stabilization of the *Textus receptus*. (henceforth T.R.). It is the intent of this paper to see to what degree Norzi's contributions aided this phenomenon and to see how they relate to the more reliable Tiberian manuscripts. His reliance on the Zohar for establishing the correct Biblical Text as well as his reverence for Menachem De Lunzano will also be examined.[2] We will also explore the methodological rules employed by Minḥat Shai in his quest to regulate the T.R., with emphasis on the consonantal text.

Norzi was born circa 1560 in Mantua, Italy to a renowned family of bankers and scholars. The Norzi family hailed from Norsa (in

---

1. For the most recent and updated bibliography to Minḥat Shai see: Maria Josefa De Azcarraga Servert, *"Minḥat Say" de Y. S. De Norzi, Profetas Menores* (Textos y Estudios "Cardenal Cisneros" 40, Madrid: C.S.I.C., 1987), pp.xi-xii. More recently see: *"Mikra", Text, Translation, Reading and Interpretation of the Hebrew Bible in Ancient Judaism and Early Christianity*, ed. Martin J. Mulder (Assen: Van Gorcum, Philadelphia: Fortress, 1988), p.122.

2. For the most recent work done on Lonzano see: Maria Teresa Ortega Monasterio, *Texto Hebreo Biblico De Sefarad En El ᵓÔr Tôrah de Měnaḥem de Lonzano* (Texto Y Estudios "Cardenal Cisneros" 25, Madrid: C.S.I.C., 1980).

Umbria) and hence their name. He was ordained as Rabbi in 1585 and sometime later served as co-Rabbi in Mantua. His main teacher was the famous kabbalist, Rabbi Moshe Cases who also happened to be his uncle.[3] Undoubtedly it was this uncle, among other factors, that acquainted Norzi with the Zohar. Well educated in the classical traditional rabbinic studies, Norzi was somehow drawn into masoretic branch of learning. His work known to us as Minḥat Shai was originally named by Norzi גודר פרץ. It was completed in 1626 (the year of his death), and circulated for many years in handwritten copies, some of which have survived.[4] His lifetime work and masterpiece was eventually printed in his home town Mantua, more than 100 years after his death, when Raphael Chaim Basilea, between 1742-1744, published the Bible Edition of Mantua with the commentary of Norzi, and named it Minḥat Shai (Shai = *Shin* for Shlomo, *Yod* for Yedidiah).[5] The introduction to this work, though vital and important, was not published until 1819 by Samuel Vita Della Volta in Pisa.[6]

In his introduction, Norzi describes his master plan, which is to produce a full masoretic worktable to the Bible. He intended to

---

3. His teachers include R. Moshe Frankita Harari and a certain R. Shlomo Abu, the cantor of the sefardic congregation in Venice. My thanks to Dr. J. Penkower, who at the oral presentation of this paper informed me that where, in the printed editions of Minḥat Shai, it seems to say R. Shlomo ibn, it is a mistake and should read Abu. See Norzi's comments to 1 Sam 25:5, where he asked his teacher a question concerning masoretic matters and received no answer.

4. These written copies are extant in the following Libraries and collections: Kaufman Collection, Budapest, #43-45; Neubauer Collection, Oxford 1444; British Museum, Margolies #231. For a Norzi autograph see British Museum Add. #27,198.

5. The dates of the Mantua print given by C.D. Ginzburg as 1732 (*Introduction to the Massoretico-Critical Edition of the Hebrew Bible* [London, 1897, reprinted New York: Ktav, 1966], p. 28), and by C. Roth as 1712-1714 (*The Jews in the Renaissance* [Philadelphia: Jewish Publication Society, 1959], p. 315), are incorrect.

6. Dr. Penkower orally expressed doubt about the existence of this particular print of Norzi's introduction.

determine its correct orthographic spelling, vocalization, accentuation, Qere-Kethib, the full gamut and scale of masoretic traditions. The reason he named his work גודר פרץ (The Fixer of the Breach), was due to the sad state of the text of the Bible. As he saw it, it was replete with various readings, plene and defective spelling, conflicting vocalizations. Norzi saw it as a Divine Duty to repair the breach. As he tells us:

ואין ראוי שיהיה בתורת ה' תמימה אפילו תג אחת או דגש א' שאין
בו סוד ולא לחנם יגעו כמה יגיעות בעלי המסורה... וכל
המתרשלים בחכמה הזאת ומבזים אותה, עליהם הכתוב אומר...

He proceeds to explain through rabbinic statements (alternating between pure Hebrew and -- should I call it Masoretic Aramaic?) the importance of the Masorah: why a correct Biblical Text is detrimental to certain rabbinic methods of Drash, and why, due to the rather famous kabbalistic teaching that the entire Torah consists of Divine Names, it is imperative that the Biblical Text be free of any mistakes.[7] Norzi goes on to tell us the importance of grammatical knowledge in determining a correct text and some of the sources and methods he will use in conjunction with his work. He also tells us of his friendship with Lunzano. He concludes with a prayer of forgiveness for any mistakes he might make and tells us that:

כי בכל כוחי ובכל מאדי מסרתי נפשי עליו לכבוד תורת ה' תמימה

from which we can surmise that he spent not only time (his lifetime) but a considerable amount of money in order to conduct his work. For example, he tells us:

ועברתי ארחות ימים למצא ספר הרמ"ה הנקרא מסורת סייג לתורה

and then he tells us:

כי גם שמלאכה זו מלאכת שמים היא, אין טוב לכלות בה כל ימים

---

7. Zohar Yitro 87a. See Nahmanides, end of introduction to Genesis, Chavel Edi. (Heb.) p.6. Also see G. G. Scholem, *On the Kabbalah and its Symbolism* pp. 37-44.

He would rather be spending his time learning Talmud and his friends urged him to cut his work short and print it. As we already know, that didn't come to fruition for another century.

Norzi, in his introduction, tells us twice:

ואקבצה מששים מחברים... וסימניך הנה מטתו שלשלמה
ששים גיבורים סביב לה

and indeed, when we count his sources (not including the standard rabbinic works like the Talmud, Midrashim, etc.), we find that he used more than 144 sources.[8] In his comments to the Torah, the most quoted work is the מסורת סייג לתורה of R. Meir Abulafia, which he, like Lunzano, followed closely. The references to the works of Radak in his entire commentary are well above 400, which shows the deep reliance of Norzi on Kimhi's grammatical rules. The wide range of sources he used extends from Azzariah Derossi's מאור עינים to Immanuel of Rome, to the standard kabbalistic works like שערי אורה and the works of M.A. Fano.

Of the many manuscripts used by Norzi, only a few have been identified. They include the famous Toledo manuscript of 1277 (now Derossi #782) a *Hilleli*, a copy of *Hilleli*, and *Sepher Ezra*.[9] His des-

---

8. The following is a partial and selected list:

אבן עזרא, אלשיך, אהב שכל, אבודרהם, אגרות שמואל, אילת אהובים, אוצר כבוד, אפודי, באר שבע, בהיר, ברית לוי, בעל הטורים, באורי איזיק שטיין, בעל התרומה, בעל מקנה אברהם, באר הגולה, בחיי, באר מים חיים, גאולת הגר, גור אריה, גינת אגוז, דרשת שלמה, דרשת אבן שועיב, דרך אמונה, דברי אגור, הלכות גדולות, הליכות עולם, היכל השם, זוהר, חזקוני, חכמת שלמה, יהודה בן בלעם, ר' יעקב לבית הלוי, יהודה מוסקתא, ר' ירוחם, יפה תואר, ספר יצירה, ילקוט, כללי הגמרא, כסף משנה, כלי יקר, ספר כריתות, לקח טוב, לשון לימודים, לב אהרון, לוית חן, מכלל יופי, מאור עינים, מראות אלקים, מאיר תהילות, מנות הלוי, מאור איוב, מטה משה, מהלך שבילי הדעות, מאיר נתיב, ספר המרכבה, מתנות כהונה, מקנה אברהם, מקור חיים, המאירי, נוה שלום, נורא תהילות, נשמת שבט הלוי, פסיקתא זוטרתי, פתח דבר, פענח רזא, צמח דוד, ציוני, קב נקי, שרש ישי, שערי אורה, תיקון ר' תם, תרומת הדשן, תורת עולם.

9. My thanks again to Dr. Penkower, who at the oral reading of this paper, informed us that, in a Master Project done at B.R.G.S. Yeshiva University in 1969 under the sponsorship of Dr. Michael Bernstein, he identified another manuscript that Norzi used; it is the B. M. Harley 5710-5711.

cription of manuscripts is wanting, in light of the hundreds of references to:

ספרי המדוייקים, במקצאת המדוייקים, ברוב המדוייקים,
ספרים חשובים, בספרי ספרד, בספרי אשכנז.

Now to describe Norzi's methodology (in his comments to the Prophets and Writings) in his attempt to stabilize the consonantal text.

1. Sometimes he cannot decide on a certain reading and leaves the matter undecided. This occurs nine (9) times.[10]

2. Many times he offers a Midrashic-Talmudic statement for Masoretic note.[11]

3. He checked the T.R. (of the Prophets and Writings) against the Targum, and dealt with some of the variant readings (translations). To this he had two approaches:

a) That indeed the Targum had a different reading. This occurs seven (7) times.[12]

b) That the Targum was only clarifying and explaining the passage:

ומה שתרגם יונתן פירושו היא.

This occurs five (5) times.[13]

4. Deviation of the T.R. in Rabbinic sources are also dealt with. This occurs twenty (20) times.[14] His approach to this problem is:

ודרך דרש נאמר, ואין משיבין על האגדה, ודרך הגמרא לקצר הפסוקים.

---

10. Josh 8:12, Isa 10:23, 2 Sam 6:23, 21:20, 2 Kgs 18:29, Ezek 13:21, Prov 8:16, Job 25:5, 2 Chron 1:17.

11. For example see: Josh 2:1, Judg 4:18, Prov 17:26 and many more.

12. Amos 3:12, Jer 11:2, 15:14, 17:2, 32:32, Ezek 5:11, 13:11.

13. 1 Sam 5:6, 1 Kgs 12:1, 2 Kgs 19:34, Ezek 27:27, Zech 8:1. See also Jer 51:18.

14. Exod 12:6, Deut 33:13, Judg 4:8, Isa 51:4, Ezek 33:12, 48:9, Amos 1:11, 4:13, Mic 4:10, Zeph 1:12, Ps 50:23, Prov 2:2, 12:25, 17:26, 24:21, Job 12:23, 36:33, Neh 4:16, Ecc 8:1, 10.

5. The Masorah is always followed when in contradiction with Rabbinic sources, as already noted by earlier halakhic authorities.[15] He also, though, did not fear to correct the Masorah itself. This occurs seven (7) times.[16]

6. At times he ventures to correct Rabbinic works. This occurs six (6) times.[17] He also amended the works of Kimhi, this occuring six (6) times.[18] He also noted variants to the T.R. from the commentary of Rashi. This occuring eight (8) times.[19] He twice corrected the text of Rashi and once set out to establish its form reliably.[20]

7. As we already stated, Norzi was very much occupied with the Divine Names. This was due to the halakhic requirements involved in writing a Divine Name and to the Kabbalistic teaching that the Biblical Text was totally comprised of Divine Names. Norzi himself tells us in his introduction that he will investigate:

והשמות אשר נפל בהן מחלוקת בין קודש לחול.

He deals with this issue no less than thirty-two (32) times.[21]

8. Norzi had access to Menachem DeLunzano's hand written comments on the margin of the Venice Rabbinic Bible. He quotes from

---

15. See Responsa of Rashba (Warsaw, 1882), no.232 (i.e. of R. Solomon ibn Aderet, d. 1310; attributed to Nahmanides), Responsa of R. Yehuda Minz (Cracow, 1882), no.8 (R. Yehuda died in 1507), and the recently published Responsa of R. Moshe Halawa (Jerusalem, 1982), no.144, (R. Moshe was a student of Rashba).

16. Jer 35:4, 44:6, Ezek 27:21, Joel 1:16, Job 23:17, Esth 8:11, 2 Chron 1:17.

17. Gen 25:23, Num 29:15, 2 Sam 21:18, Ezek 31:15, Hos 8:1, Dan 2:22.

18. 2 Sam 17:2, Isa 9:5, Jer 8:1, 22:13, Ezek 8:3, Job 9:24.

19. Isa 27:3, 28:25, 35:7, 36:2, Ezek 38:16, Zech 12:10, Prov 21:6, 1 Chron 17:9.

20. He corrects the text in Isa 37:24, Prov 29:13, and sets out to find a reliable form in Gen 14:14.

21. Gen 1:27, 18:3, 19:2, 19:18, 20:3, 31:59, 33:10, 35:7, Deut 32:39, 2 Sam 7:22, 12:25, 1 Kgs 3:15, 21:8, Isa 10:16, 13:6, Jer 23:6, Ezek 48:35, Hos 9:8, 12:7, 14:1, Ps 1:7, 50:1, 82:1, 84:8, 90:17, Job 16:11, 19:22, 22:25, Dan 2:34, 4:16, Cant 1:1, 2 Chron 35:21.

these notes twenty-two (22) times, and only disagrees with Lunzano five (5) times.[22] His attitude to Lunzano can best be described using his own words:

וכדאי הוא אותו זקן לסמוך עליו דודאי דק ואשכח הכי בספרים דוקני

Yet, if he felt that Lunzano was incorrect, Norzi followed his own way.

9. The basic methodology employed by Norzi in his collation of texts and manuscripts is explained in his own introduction:

ונתתי לבי לחקור אחר הספרים... והחשובים והמעולים שראוי
לסמוך עליהם ולנטות בהם אחר הרוב בדרך שנצטוינו מן התורה
אחרי רבים להטות במו שעשו חכמים בג' ספרים שמצאו בעזרה

In other words his approach had two components:

a) the use of reliable manuscripts
b) the rule of the majority.

Norzi stuck to these rules as he tells us: ובטל יחיד במיעוטו, ואמנם ברוב הספרים. He followed the majority of reliable manuscripts in seventeen (17) cases he describes.[23] This does not take into account the numerous times he states without any explanation: ברוב המדוייקים.[24]

---

22. He quotes in Gen 3:7, 2 Sam 6:23, 2 Kgs 20:13, Isa 10:15, Jer 31:37, Ezek 44:12, Mic 2:2, Zech 3:10, Prov 8:16, Ps 1:1, 17:4, 43:1, 39:13, 44:19, 55:22, 105:36, Esth 9:2. He disagress only in Job 6:21, Ezra 8:22, Neh 3:31, 12:37, 2 Chron 10:14.

23. 1 Kgs 2:20, 15:21, 2 Kgs 8:25, 24:20, Isa 7:15, 59:18, Jer 23:8, 23:27, Zech 7:1, Nah 3:9, Ezek 18:16, 24:17, 37:11, Prov 7:26, 28:17, Ezra 10:14, 2 Chron 10:14.

24. In the new Tanach editions issued by Mosad Ha-Rav Kook, with the commentary of *Daat Mikra*, along with each volume there is a masoretic compendium, verse by verse, comparing the more reliable Tiberian Manuscripts to the Rabbinic Bible of Yaakov B. Chaim. This important work is being done by R. M. Breuer. When collating to this compendium the comments of Norzi, in those instances where Norzi quoted two opinions or two manuscripts, R. M. Breuer has placed a question mark next to Norzi's name, thus showing the uncertainty of Norzi's intentions. In the light of what we said, when Norzi does quote two opinions, if he identifies one of them as מדוייקים or חשובים, it is his intention that the Biblical Text should read as such. I would even venture to say that when Norzi uses the phrase במקצת המדוייקים, it was also his intention for the text to read as

As we already stated, Norzi sometimes left the issue undecided. In speaking about ספרים מדויקים, it should be pointed out that in 99% of the instances where Norzi uses this phrase it finds a parallel in the more reliable Tiberian manuscripts, in reference to the consonantal text (the Kethib). Only once when using this phrase, its parallel is not found, This occurs at Proverbs 28:3:

גבר רש וַעשק — בספרים דוקני בלא וא"ו

10. Norzi (similarly Lunzano) used the Zohar as a source for establishing the correct Biblical Text.In his masoretic comments to the Torah alone, Norzi quotes the Zohar fifty (50) times.[25] On eleven (11) of these occasions, the Biblical Text of the Zohar has a variant reading.[26] Differing from Lunzano, who at times tried to fit the Zoharic version to the T.R., Norzi states in all eleven (11) places that we follow the Masorah. One example will suffice:

"כלו" ובזוהר דשיר השירים נראה שהיא בה"א בסוף תיבה
ובעל אור תורה נדחק לפרשו, ולא יתחויאר אצלי, וכבר
הודעתי פעמים רבות דקים לן כמסורת

We should point out that in one instance he expresses his doubt, wondering how it is a book of such holiness contains deviant readings, but in the end, the Masorah wins out.[27] In his comments to the Prophets and the Writings, Norzi quotes the Zohar fifty-four (54) times

---

such. Norzi was systematically and indeed eclectically establishing (or correcting) what he believed was the Masoretic Text. This explains the reason so many times he confirmed from manuscripts a reading which was never questioned.

25. Gen 1:14 (8 times), 1:21, 2:4, 2:22, 6:3, 4, 13:3, 19:33, 20:6, 24:14, 33:4, Exod 3:4, 12:16, 14:7, 19 at the end of chapter, 23:15, 24:10, 25:23, Lev 1:1, 7:11, 9:43, 21:5, 26:3, 26:42, Num 6:23, 7:1, 9:10, 9:11, 13:22, 15:35, 19:2, 21:34, 21:35, 23:9, 24:2, 25:11. Deut 6:4, 6:8, 11:12, 22:19, 32:6, 32:39, 32:40.

26. Exod 14:7, 23:15, 25:22, Lev 7:11, Num 9:10, 21:34, 35, 23:9, 24:2, 25:11, Deut 22:2, 30.

27. Num. 23:9.

and with the same approach.[28] It should be pointed out that at times he uses the Zohar to back up a reliable Tiberian reading. In one instance, concering a Divine Name, Norzi "was mislead" (if we might use such a phrase). Two verses in Psalms have similar wording:

לכו חזו מפעלות י-ה-ו-ה (Ps 46:9)

לכו חזו מפעלות א-ל-ה-י-ם (Ps 66:5)

He introduces the problem with the words: זה אחד מן המקראות הקשין לי במקרא. His dilema is at Ps 46:9, where he wonders if the text should read י-ה-ו-ה, or if אלהים, as in Ps 66:5. At Ps 66:5, there is no problem since all the manuscripts and prints read אלהים. Quoting early prints, and some other sources (including כתבי יד מדויקים) that read י-ה-ו-ה at Ps 46:9, Norzi tells us that the Zohar (at Genesis 47a) contains an exposition explaining why the name אלהים is used at 46:9. After some deliberation with other sources, he finally decides in favor of אלהים at Ps 46:9. Had he stuck to his own methodology of following המדויקים, Norzi would agree with the more reliable Tiberian manuscripts, but some manuscripts and the exposition of the Zohar led him the other way.

While Norzi, in conjuction with Lunzano and R. Meir Abulafia (RAMAH) have more or less determined the T.R. of the last few hundred years (before Kennicot, DeRossi) in relation to Torah, yet with regard to the Prophets and the Writings, Norzi in his Minḥat Shai, was the only one. In order to see the extent of his influence, we decided to check one edition that printed the work of Norzi along with the Biblical Text, and see to what degree the editors followed his advice. We have chosen the famous Lublin edition, used widely today as the מקראות גדולות, complete with the classical medieval rabbinic commentators. It

---

28. Josh 22:22 (twice), Judg 6:24, 17:7, 20:18, 1 Sam 2;9, 17:23, 2 Sam 22:47, 1 Kgs 12:16 (twice), 17:14, 20:20, Isa 9:6, 13:6, 38:11, 48:11, 42:24, 43:14, 51:4, 55:8, 57:2, 58:7, 63:9, Jer 2:3 (twice), Ezek 1:1, Zeph 1:9 (6 times), Zech 1:10, 9:9, Mal 2:15, Ps 21:2, 24:4 (twice) 29:8, 30:1, 37:28, 42:9, 46:9, 48:14, 84:12, 100:3, 104:35 (twice) 106:2, 145:10 (twice), Prov 2:2 (twice), 11:26, 22:3, 23:24.

was printed in Lublin by the team of Moshe Schneidmesser and
Nechama Hirshhorn in 1887 and the following ten years. They indeed
advertised their edition as מדויק היטב על פי המסורה. Here again, we
are only referring to the consonantal text. In fact, the editors ignored
Norzi's comments in over 270 places, even though they printed his
work on the same page with the Biblical Text.[29]

A short word is in order concerning the works written as commentaries on the Minḥat Shai. Two minor works were written, both on
the Minḥat Shai of the Five Scrolls. One, named שירי מנחה, was written by Shraga Phoebus b. Solomon of Dubrowna and printed in Shklov
in 1800.[30] The second one, named באר שבע, was written by Moshe
Arye b. Zev, Rabbi of Trestin and printed in 1845. The third and more
famous work is the אור החיים, written by R. Haim b. Zev Bender of
Vilna, and printed in the same city in 1867.[31] This work received the
approbation of the rabbis of the time, including the approbation of R.

---

29. I give here only a partial list. Norzi's reading is underlined in each case.
The complete list, including the comparison to the Tiberian manuscripts and
Genizah fragments will be dealt with at some other time.

Joshua 1:15 (המה – הם), 3:4 (שלשום – שלשם), 6:23 (ויצאו – ויציאו), 8:22
למשפחת 21:26 (ושמנים – ושמונים), 14:10 (בעשתרות – בעשתרת), 9:10 (להם – לו)
למשפחות (–).

Judges 8:27 (אותו – אתו), 9:7 (ויגדו – ויגידו), 13:25 (אשתול – אשתאל), 15:14
צידנים (–) 18:7 (חללנו – חללינו), 16:24 (המזוזות – המזוזת), 16:3 (זרעותיו – זרעותיו)
צדנים 21:8 (מיביש – מיבש).

30. The approbation of R. Shlomo Zalman Chuna of Dubrowna includes
the following comment:

הגם כי זכינו לספר מנחת שי אשר היטב לדבר גם בנ״ך עם כל זה לא פירש אפילו אחד
ממאה ופרץ מרובה על העומד [!].

31. Mistakenly identified by some as R. Haim Zev, but correctly read Haim
ben Zev. His professional activity was that of a Torah-scribe. This book also comments on the שירי מנחה. Also see the approbations in the book which contain
lavish praise placed upon Norzi for his masoretic masterpiece. The author tells us
that it took him 18 years to complete his work.

Naftali Tzvi Yehuda Berlin (Netziv). It consists of 36 pages and in total comments on 374 of Norzi's notations.

We have said nothing of the poetic style of Norzi, of his many corrections to the Bible printed in Pesaro in 1520, with the commentary of Abravanel which was full of printing errors, so that Norzi stopped it in its tracks; nothing of the personality that emerges from his work. At times you feel his frustration and you sense his dilligent hard work. In other words, his legacy lives on and still needs to be studied, and that at some other time and place.

# THE DISCREPANCIES BETWEEN
## MOSHE AND AHARON BEN-ASHER

Saul Levin
State University of New York at Binghamton

Long after I learned from Paul Kahle[1] and others about the great Ben-Asher family of Masoretes in Tiberias, culminating in Aharon ben-Moshe ben-Asher, I had occasion to wonder how it happened that this Aharon differed in some noteworthy details from his father. I do not mean differences merely in notation; e.g., that Aharon much oftener than Moshe omitted the רפי stroke above the letters בגדכפת to show fricativation. For nearly all the punctators treated this mark as more or less optional, except on the first letter of a word in a conjuncture such as לֹא־עָשׂוּ כֵן 'they did not do so' (Judges 2:17).[2] Elsewhere, as in the very next word וְכִי־ 'And when', whether they made the רפי stroke with their pen (as Moshe did) or like Aharon they neglected to make it, anyhow they certainly gave the letter a relaxed or

---

1. First in his *Masoreten des Westens*, I (Stuttgart: W. Kohlhammer, 1927; repr. Hildesheim: Georg Olms 1967):1-18.

2. The excellent Codex 115 of the 2d Firkovich Collection in St. Petersburg omits the רפי only if a superscript accent occurs on the same letter — and not even then if that letter begins a word; see my article, "Defects, Alleged or Real, in the Tiberias Pointing," *Hebrew Studies* 23 (1983):74, and *The Indo-European and Semitic Languages: An exploration of structural similarities related to accent, chiefly in Greek, Sanskrit, and Hebrew* (Albany: State University of New York Press, 1971): 224. Also the Kaufmann codex of the Mishna, which has no accents, omits the רפי only on ה at the end of a word; Georg Beer (ed.), *Faksimile-Ausgabe des Mischnacodex Kaufmann A 50* (Haag: M. Nijhoff, 1929; repr. Jerusalem תשב״ח).

fricative sound [k̲]; otherwise they would have marked it with a dot, the דגש, to show the stronger or plosive sound [k].

But there are real, though not gross differences in how Aharon and Moshe ben-Asher pronounced words in the sacred text. Two of those differences turn up in a frequent word, בְּיִשְׂרָאֵל according to Aharon but בִּישְׂרָאֵל according to Moshe. In both respects Aharon's treatment has prevailed. Such variation is interesting for several reasons — among them, the special light it throws upon a general problem of linguistics, to pin down the way that the pronunciation of a language gradually changes. Here we have the special circumstance of an ancient language being perpetuated by meticulous, conservative readers, whose paramount concern was to transmit the מקרא of the holy books exactly as they had learned it in their youth. Unlike other people in more ordinary circumstances of using a language, they were quite disinclined to modify or up-date anything in their Hebrew tradition, out of deference to the language that they heard spoken around them, or in compliance with contemporary speech-habits.

Even so, they were obviously in daily contact with the current Aramaic vernacular of the Jewish community in Tiberias, and no doubt conversant to some extent with Arabic too; for the Arabs had been in control of the entire region for more than two hundred years. The Masoretic notes upon the Bible codices are couched in very succinct Aramaic. The colophons at the end, including the one written by Moshe ben-Asher himself, are in ordinary post-Biblical Hebrew, with plenty of Scriptural phrases, but otherwise little if any attempt to recapture the syntax or spelling of Biblical Hebrew. In their role as expert readers of holy Scripture, they were determined to keep the מקרא as they had received it. The impact of anything else upon it was to be minimal, if not absolutely nil.

They accomplished this not by thoughtless memorization and parroting, but by the most attentive and intellectual concentration upon the exact sound of each word in the text. This might vary from one occurrence of a word to another, as the Hebrew for 'your wife' is אֶשְׁתְּךָ in Psalm 128 (at the beginning of verse 3) but אִשְׁתְּךָ everywhere else in the corpus. In any one passage, however, it ought not to vary from one competent reader to another — no more than a word of variable spelling, such as נב(י)אים 'prophets', might be written either way in a given passage by two competent scribes.[3] On the contrary, the Masoretic method was to keep track of all the inconsistencies in the text tradition and maintain them — far from settling upon one norm for the Hebrew language and applying it uniformly throughout the text.

But notwithstanding all their effort to read the text identically every time, and to preserve all of its internal divergences, the readers were not identical with one another. The discrepancies between the Ben-Asher reading and the Ben-Naphtali reading attracted the notice of Jewish scholars outside of Tiberias, and during the middle ages they made lists of items like וְנֹאכֲלֶנּוּ 'and let's eat him' according to Ben-Asher but וְנֹאכְלֶנּוּ according to Ben-Naphtali, in II Kings 6:28-29 (a gruesome episode during the siege of Samaria). Several other forms of the verb 'eat', with this masculine object-suffix (or with the feminine ‎נָּ֫הָ‎ -), undergo the same variation within the root between the weak vowel [ă] and the colorless vocalic glide [ə].[4] Both readings are attested in later codices. However, we in modern times unfortunately have no codex containing a direct attribution to the Ben-Naphtali family or school.

If all the discrepancies between the Tiberias readers were so minor as וְנֹאכֲלֶנּוּ/וְנֹאכְלֶנּוּ, we would be tempted to put them aside, with only the conclusion that no difference in sound — not even a nearly subliminal one — was too minute for a Masoretic ear to catch, and for a Masoretic mind to dwell upon. But there are discrepancies that make somewhat more impact upon our ears, and they show up between individual men with the surname Ben-Asher — as I have said, בִּישְׂרָאֵל Moshe ben-Asher, but בְּיִשְׂרָאֵל Aharon. The medieval lists do not recognise Moshe ben-Asher as an authority separate from Aharon; rather they attribute to Ben-Naphtali the form with בִּי֫שְׂ- at the beginning in-

---

3. See my review of J. Barr, *The Variable Spellings of the Hebrew Bible*, in *General Linguistics* 31 (1991):189.

4. C. D. Ginsburg, *Introduction to the Massoretico-critical Edition of the Hebrew Bible* (London: Trinitarian Bible Society, 1897; repr. New York: Ktab, 1966): 255-264.

stead of ‑בְּיָשׁ. And וּנֹאכְלֶנּוּ, which according to them is the Ben-
Naphtali form, is also in the great Cairo codex of Moshe ben-Asher.

The muddle has prompted a few scholars, beginning with Adolf
Neubauer,[5] to discredit the colophon of this codex, which contains the
Former and the Latter Prophets. That colophon begins
אני משה בן אשר כתבתי זה המחזור שלמקרא 'I, Moshe ben-Asher,
have written this volume of the Reading....'[6] It goes on to state the
year 827 from the destruction of the Second Temple. The penmanship
of the colophon is the same as that of the sacred text; so a critic — or
rather, a hyper-critic — who attacks the genuineness of this codex is
bound to posit that some nameless scribe and punctator has assumed a
false identity, presumably in order to sell at a higher price the copy
which he must have labored long and hard to produce. Such hyper-
criticism is a disease of modern scholarship, which professes to invalid-
ate a large part of the primary evidence instead of making the utmost
use of it. Any good critic must indeed **observe** wherein the witnesses
disagree; but in the field of philology or history, true criticism ought
not to be mistaken for a legal process, in which a judge is obliged to
pronounce a verdict at the end — either upholding or rejecting one side
of the case.

Hyper-criticism sometimes does more harm than just misleading
the critic himself and those who follow him — until eventually the illu-
sion is dispelled, with or without an explicit, cogent refutation by
someone else. Permanent material harm can result meanwhile, as we
have seen all too well in the case of the Aleppo codex, which — according to the colophon — was pointed and Masoretically annotated by
Aharon ben-Asher. William Wickes in the nineteenth century discredit-
ed this claim because a specimen page, which was photographed for
him, revealed a conflict between the punctator's use of the מֵתֶג and the

---

5. "The Introduction of the Square Characters in Biblical Mss. and an Account
of the Earliest Mss. of the Old Testament," *Studia Biblica et Ecclesiastica*, 3 (Oxford,
1891):25. Cf. Kahle (above, note 1):16-17.

6. A photographic facsimile (unfortunately of rather poor quality) was published
by D. S. Loewinger (Jerusalem: Makor, 1970):
תנ׳ך כתב יד קאהיר ... נכתב בשנת 895 על ידי משה בן אשר

rules for it in the later medieval treatise דקדוקי הטעמים, attributed to Aharon ben-Asher. So Wickes judged the Aleppo codex to be worthless for his purpose;[7] and the opportunity to have it photographed, or least collated from beginning to end, was allowed to slip away. No later scholar had access to it, till after it suffered grievous damage in the riot of 1947. Now we have substantial remains of Aharon's handiwork, so as to look up his authoritative treatment of the מקרא, but much less than the entire codex of all twenty-four books.[8]

Accepting the codices as authentic, what are we to do with discrepancies such as בְּיִשְׂרָאֵל/בִּישְׂרָאֵל? We have them both on good though not necessarily equal authority. That both readings had standing in the learned community of Tiberias is more important, at least from a linguistic point of view, than the names of the authorities. The variation itself is of intrinsic interest, as proof of something unsettled about the ancient Hebrew language which had come down through the מקרא.

Aharon ben-Asher was certainly younger than Moshe. So we are surprised that Aharon did not simply learn and repeat Moshe's pronunciation — particularly if he was Moshe's son. That relationship, however, is not stated in the Aleppo codex (where we would expect it) nor of course in the Cairo codex (produced by Moshe when Aharon was presumably quite young); but in the colophon of the Leningrad or St. Petersburg codex B 19a of the entire תנ׳׳ך, copied by שמואל בן יעקב early in the eleventh century; we are told that he checked it against the books pointed by אהרן בן משה בן אשר. The plural ספרים, if used carefully, signifies that Shemuel consulted at least two codices pointed

---

7. *A Treatise on the Accentuation of the Twenty-one So-called Prose Books of the Old Testament* (Oxford: Clarendon Press, 1887):vii-ix.

8. The premise of the hyper-critics, that the colophons in Hebrew Bible codices are likely to be spurious, was based on an amazingly loose generalization. In the nineteenth century one energetic but unscrupulous Karaite scholar, Firkovich, before selling to the imperial library in St. Petersburg the old codices that he had collected, did in fact forge small changes in some colophons so as to make them out a few hundred years older than they really were. But his tampering was easily detected and does not affect the true worth of those codices — let alone the many others that he never touched.

by Aharon; so he may have read אהרן בן משה בן אשר (or the like) in the colophon of one — if not more than one. Or it is possible that he merely inferred it from the gap in age — real or supposed — between Aharon and Moshe.

The colophon of the Aleppo codex climaxes a most laudatory description of Aharon by giving his name in this form, מר רב אהרן בן מר רב אשר, followed by a well-known formula that proves he was dead by that time. The occasion for writing this colophon was not the completion of the codex but the subsequent donation of it to a certain synagogue. Neither is any date given; that the codex was made early in the tenth century — as Kahle and others have figured — is likely enough, but not a plain fact on a par with the dating of the Cairo codex and many others.

The absence of Moshe's name in that colophon poses a problem, which we lack the means to solve. But no matter how he was related to Aharon — perhaps as older brother or half-brother — both of them were authorities in Tiberias. The colophons assure us of that. Where the two authorities diverge, we are scarcely in a position to judge in favor of one. The later scribes and punctators did in practice commit themselves, one way or the other; and their practice is of linguistic import, as I will explain at the close of the paper.

By pronouncing בִּישְׂרָאֵל and marking the letters accordingly, Moshe ben-Asher went a little beyond two phonological rules of Hebrew that we can extract from the Tiberias מקרא otherwise: (a) The prefixes -בְּ 'in', -לְ 'to', and -כְּ 'like' take the vowel [i] only if the following consonant takes the minimal vowel-sound [ə]; e.g. before the mythical place שְׁאוֹל, yielding בִּשְׁאוֹל. When the following consonant is [y-], as in יְהוּדָה, it gets absorbed into the vowel [i]: בִּיהוּדָה. Moshe extended this treatment to words that begin not with [yə-] but with [yi-]. Thus, when the infinitive יִרְאָה is prefixed, his pointing of 'to fear' is לִירְאָה, in contrast to Aharon's לְיִרְאָה (I Kings 8:43). Likewise וּבִישְׁרַת לֵבָב 'and in uprightness of heart' (3:6; וּבְיִשְׁרַת לֵבָב Aharon), and the place-name בִּיזְרְעֶאל (21:1; בְּיִזְרְעֶאל Aharon). Moshe did not apply this to the prefix that means 'and' — thus וְיִשְׂרָאֵל (Joshua 22:22, etc.) — nor to the 'from' prefix — מִיִשְׂרָאֵל (Judges 20:13). Nor, with the other prefixes, does the reduc-

tion of two initial syllables to one in בִּישְׂרָאֵל, etc., entail a lengthening of the vowel [i]: בִּישְׂרָאֵל (I Sam. 26:15), כִּישְׂרָאֵל 'like Israel'
(II Sam. 7:23), לִישְׂרָאֵל (Joshua 8:22) — not even with the accent
זקף or פשטא, the ones that are most often preceded by מתג within the
same word (as in לִיהוּדָה, בֵּיהוּדָה, II Kings 23:26, 18:22).

(b) Moshe's רפי above the א in יְשְׂרָאֵל shows weakening of this consonant, the glottal stop — whether or not to the extreme of impercepti-
bility. This differs from the phonology of Biblical Hebrew as given
otherwise; if not for his יְשְׂרָאֵל, we could simply state that the glottal
stop **between vowels** is always maintained intact. But his pronunciation, weakening or dropping the glottal stop between vowels in this
very familiar proper name, ought not to surprise any professional pho-
netician. For as Witold Mańczak has thoroughly demonstrated for languages in general, the sounds in an especially frequent word are more
liable to erosion than in other words;[9] and besides, the glottal stop is
by nature the least articulate of consonants and so the most prone to
succumb. A similar phonetic environment is present in חֲזָאֵל, the king
of Syria; but here Moshe gives us the normal א. We cannot tell what he
would have done with several other names — רְפָאֵל, מִישָׁאֵל, מִיכָאֵל
— which do not occur in the eight books; would he make it [-ɔʔé-] in
these, like חֲזָאֵל, or [-ɔé-], like יְשְׂרָאֵל?

In another comparable name, however, he — along with others
— manifests this weakening or disappearance of the glottal stop between the vowels [i] and [é]. That is דֱּנָאֵל in Ezekiel 14:14,20, where
Aharon has דֱּנִאֵל (in 28:3 מִדֱּנִאֵל). Although Aharon's Masoretic
note in the margin does not (as the Leningrad codex does) categorize
these passages in Ezekiel as the קרי — namely דניאל — conflicting
with the כתיב, Aharon's דגש belongs to the missing letter '; and so we
find it written in I Chronicles 3:1 דֱּנִיֵּאל, where the name recurs as
David's son by Abigail. No doubt the Aleppo codex of Aharon had this
spelling and pointing in the book of Daniel likewise. Certainly the Leningrad codex has it there: the letter ' marked strong with דגש, and

---

9. *Le développement phonétique des langues romanes et la fréquence* (Kraków:
Prace Językoznawcze, 1969), *Frequenzbedingter unregelmäßiger Lautwandel in den
germanischen Sprachen* (Wrocław: Zakad Narodowy im. Ossolinskich, 1987), etc.

the אֹ marked often (though not consistently) with רפ׳. In the same book, however, the angel is גַּבְרִיאֵל (8:16, 9:21), with a firm glottal stop unlike the name of the main character — notwithstanding the similar phonetic (and morphological) environment. The Aleppo codex probably agreed with this also, but it can be confirmed only if the missing page or pages come to light.[10]

We sense an **uneven tendency** in proper names to weaken the glottal stop in the latter component that means 'God'. At one extreme is יִשְׁמָעֵאל, in which the Tiberias text — while writing the אֹ — uniformly treats it as a null for purposes of pronunciation. For, coming right after the stronger guttural consonant ע in this name, אֹ loses its specific identity; and the vowel of the previous syllable, being now unchecked, gets actualized as [ɔ], rather than [a]. When not compounded into a personal name, the verb and noun are pointed אֵל ׀ יִשְׁמַע 'God hears' (Job 27:9, 35:13); the vertical line, called פֶּסֶק, was inserted by the punctators to mark an interruption of the conjuncture between verb and subject and thus to make the אֹ distinctly pronounceable after the ע.

Moshe's יִשְׂרָאֵל is at the other extreme, attested by only one Masoretic authority in Tiberias. I regard it as a valuable variant, indicating a pronunciation that may go back many centuries. As [yisrɔél] and [yisrɔʔél] coexisted in that community during the golden age of the punctators, both of them may have long pre-existed in the mouths of earlier generations. That either pronunciation was a recent development, is unlikely; but we lack earlier written evidence about such delicate phonetic details.

For a historical understanding of how changes in pronunciation succeed or fail, it is highly significant that when Jewry outside of Tiberias accepted the Tiberias text, the phonologically normal [yisrɔʔél] prevailed over the anomalous [yisrɔél], and the normal [bəyisrɔʔél, ləyir-

---

10. According to widespread rumors, some former members of the destroyed synagogue, who now live in Israel, managed to salvage quite a few pages that had come loose from the codex, and they keep them as valued relics safely hidden in their homes.

ʔɔ], etc., prevailed over the anomalous [bisrɔél, lirʔɔ]. Therein Moshe's authority lost out; but in וְנֹאכְלֶנּוּ and related forms of this verb, outside Jewry preferred his pointing to Aharon's וְנֹאכֲלֶנּוּ. Here too, the principle behind that preference is essentially the same: the weak vowel with the definite quality [ă] is normal only after a guttural consonant. Furthermore, right in between the two occurrences of וּנֹאכְלֹנוּ, comes the preterite וַנֹּאכְלֵהוּ 'and we ate him', and here Aharon agrees with Moshe that it is [kə], not [kă]. Whatever phonetic motive may have prompted this very fine distinction on the part of Aharon, it was bound to be regarded by most of the subsequent punctators as a futile incoherence. No reason appears for the weak [ă] between two non-guttural consonants.

As these oddities of either Aharon or Moshe were deviant phonologically, if adopted they were bound to render the Tiberias notation more difficult for anyone to master. The notation was the most thorough and accurate ever devised for the human voice, in order to capture in ink the very sounds of the Biblical Hebrew and Aramaic text. The language, as embodied in the מקרא, indeed has innumerable complexities to be grappled with. The most marginal of the alternative forms, however, exemplified by Moshe's בִּישְׂרָאֵל and Aharon's וְנֹאכֲלֶנּוּ, were afterwards likely to be rejected in practice by the Hebraists in medieval Jewry, but not forgotten.

# PARALLEL REALIZATIONS OF DICHOTOMY PATTERNS IN BIBLICAL ACCENTUATION

Rachel Mashiah
Bar-Ilan University

In the biblical accentuation every verse is divided into two parts by an appropriate disjunctive accent, and each "half-verse" is further subdivided and so on. This division, termed "continuous dichotomy", continues until the size of a minimal two words section is reached. It reveals the hierarchy of the disjunctives, since each disjunctive is determined to fit the unit it divides, and its location therein.[1]

According to the principle of "continuous dichotomy" it would be expected that segments with identical divisional structure would be accentuated similarly, however this is frequently not the case. We can find many segments that are divided in the same manner, yet differ in their accentuation. For example Gen 36,39:

וַיָּמָת בַּעַל חָנָן בֶּן-עַכְבּוֹר ֠/ וַיִּמְלֹךְ תַּחְתָּיו הֲדַר וְשֵׁם עִירוֹ פָּעוּ

In this case Segol comes at the sixth word before Etnaḥ (בֶּן עַכְבּוֹר), but in the parallel verse, I Chron 1,50, Zaqef appears at the same place (namely, at the sixth word before Etnaḥ):

---

1. The principle of continuous dichotomy is elaborated in Wickes 1881 (chapters IV and V).

וִימָת בַּעַל חָנָן // וַיִּמְלֹךְ תַּחְתָּיו הֲדַד וְשֵׁם עִירוֹ פָּעִי

Accentuational segments identical in their divisional structure and terminating disjunctive, yet differing in their accentuation, are termed Parallel Patterns.

Very few attempts have been made to clarify the phenomenon of Parallel Patterns, and so far the explanations given with respect to the phenomenon are insufficient.[2] Furthermore, there is an inclination to dismiss unsatisfactory findings as dependent upon unexplored musical elements,[3] or simply to state that the phenomenon is not rule-governed.[4] This approach is well understood, taking into account the fact that the findings so far revealed, emerged in the process of other studies of biblical accentuation, and were mainly based on personal impression.

The phenomenon of Parallel Patterns was checked in a thorough research in the twenty one Prose-Books (as a dissertation under the supervision of Prof. Aron Dotan). The purpose of our research was to give a full description of Parallel Patterns, and to reveal the variables, responsible for the existence of Parallel Patterns. On this ground it was possible to formulate new rules as well as to elaborate existing ones.[5] Such a study was naturally based upon statistic data. I have chosen to present here several characteristics of Parallel Patterns by describing some of the problems a researcher dealing with them may confront.

Such a research could not have possibly succeeded, had we not used the computer, since locating all the Parallel Patterns requires a repetitive reading of the text. For this purpose the data were gleaned

---

2. For example, the rule of Luzatto and Wickes concerning the use of Zaqef or Tipeḥa on the second word before Silluq or Etnaḥ referred to below.

3. See for instance Wickes' discussion concerning Revia and Pashta at the second word before Zaqef (Wickes 1887, p. 77).

4. See for instance Weil 1982 (p. XL).

5. Most of which were formulated by Wickes 1887.

from a computerized biblical text, based on the renowned Leningrad Codex B19a, which is located at the computer center of the "Responsa Project" at Bar-Ilan University.[6] These data were compared when necessary with the facsimile edition of the manuscript,[7] and printed editions based on it.[8]

Computer search differs considerably from a regular search, for the computer must be "taught" some basic concepts. For example:

The term "domain" -- According to the accentuation system, the domain of a certain disjunctive includes the word it appears in, as well as all those preceding words which are accentuated by conjunctives, or by disjunctives weaker than itself. Therefore the computer has to be "taught" to recognize disjunctives in contrast with conjunctives, and to identify the hierarchy of the disjunctives and their location in the verse.

The term "long word" -- According to biblical accentuation, a word is a minimal linguistic form which has one main stress. Therefore words that are combined by Maqqaf (hyphen) are considered to be one word. A long word (according to Wickes 1887, p.62) has at least two vowels preceding the main stress.[9] For example:

יִשְׂרָאֵל; עַל-פָּנָיו; וְאֶת-הַשָּׁמַ֫יִם; לִירוּשָׁלַ֫יִם

The computer must be "taught" to recognize the main stress, and to identify the word with relation to the number of vowels preceding it.

The computer must also be "taught" to identify problematic accents like Munaḥ-Legarmeh as opposed to Munaḥ + Paseq. In order

---

6. Computer programs specially designed by an expert to suit each pattern, were written according to our requests. The computer output included only the relevant occurrences of each pattern (organized according to book, chapter and verse order of the Bible), and this formed the basis of the examination.

7. תורה נביאים וכתובים, כתב-יד לנינגרד B19a..., ירושלים תשל״א.

8. R. Kittel - P. Kahle (eds), Biblia Hebraica³. Stuttgart 1937; K. Elliger - W. Rudolph (eds), Biblia Hebraica Stuttgartensia. Stuttgart 1969; א' דותן [עורך], תורה נביאים וכתובים³, מדויקים היטב... בידי אהרן דותן, תל-אביב תשמ״ו.

9. Sheva is not counted, except sheva mobile which follows a so-called long vowel as in שָׁמְרוּ.

to do that, the computer has to learn the positions in which Munaḥ-Legarmeh may occur.

Preliminary analysis of the findings made it possible to come up with some assumptions, regarding certain variables as linked to the existence of Parallel Patterns. In order to confirm or refute these assumptions in the early stages of the research, the computer was asked to classify the material with respect to each assumed variable separately. Yet very often this analysis proved to be futile, since at the most we managed to trace several tendencies, or partial explanations. It could be said, according to this analysis, that there is a tendency to accentuate those verses that have a certain characteristic in common similarly, yet no valid rules could be deduced on the basis of this tendency.

Indeed, one of the reasons for the partial rules formulated in the literature on the subject is that the examination of the material was mostly based upon a single variable. An example of this is Luzzatto's well known rule (1852 p.70), rephrased by Wickes (1887 p.62), concerning the appearance of Zaqef and Tipeḥa at the second word before Silluq and Etnaḥ. For instance, Wickes states with regard to the accentuation in the domain of the Silluq, that "when Silluq's word or the word preceding it is long, Zaqeph is admissible instead of Tiphcha, and is indeed generally preferred."

Since they examined nothing but the length of the words, they could only come up with a one way rule, describing those instances in which accentuation with Zaqef is possible. Yet on this ground it is impossible to formulate an inverse rule, for Tipeḥa may occur under these same conditions as well. In other words, Parallel Patterns do exist when one or both words to the left of the division-place are long.

It is worthwhile to add that similar distribution of these verses was found by a computer search: Tipeḥa occurs in 45% of the cases (with at least one long word to the left of the division-place), and Zaqef in 55%.

The rules so far formulated, as well as the partial rules raised in the beginning of our research, led us to the conclusion that every pattern is characterized by a compound of variables. Only by understanding the interrelation of these variables can we trace the features of each pattern, and clarify the accentuation (including abnormal or ambivalent accentuation). This can be demonstrated in three-word units, in which there is a division at the second word before Revia.

The accentuation in these units is conditioned by the length of the word at the division-place (henceforth: division-word)[10], as well as the length of the words to its left:

Munaḥ-Legarmeh is preferred in short division-words stressed on the first syllable. For example:

בְּיָדִי דָוִד עַבְדִּי (II Sam 3,18).

כִּי מַעֲלֵה הַלּוּחִית (Isa 15,5).

In contrast, Geresh (or Gershayim)[11] is preferred in long division-words (with at least two vowels before the main stress). For example:

וְאַחֲרֵי־כֵן יָצָא אָחִיו (Gen 25,26).

וַיִּתְּנוּ־קוֹל בִּיהוּדָה וּבִירוּשָׁלָ֑ם (II Chron 24,9).

As for the length of the words to the left of the division-place, it was found that Geresh is preferred before long words. For example:

לְיַדּוֹת אֶת־קַרְנוֹת הַגּוֹיִם (Zech 2,4).

In the light of the above rules, and taking into consideration the interrelationsip of the variables, it is obvious that Geresh is preferred in a long division-word followed by two long words, since the two vari-

---

10. Rules concerning the length of the division-word appear in Wickes 1887 (p. 94); Spanier 1927 (p. 23); Breuer 1982 (p. 53), yet they are inaccurately formulated.

11. Gershayim is a variant of Geresh. For the conditions under which it appears, see, for instance, Wickes, 1887, p. 112. In this paper, the name "Geresh" applies to both Geresh and Gershayim.

ables share the same tendency, and in both Geresh is preferred. (This is demonstrated in II Chron 24,9 above).

However, the accentuation is not at all clear in units where two long words follow a short division-word stressed on the first syllable, since the two variables have opposing tendencies: on the one hand there is a tendency to accentuate this unit with Munaḥ-Legarmeh, for the division-word is stressed on the first syllable; while on the other hand Geresh is preferred before long words. The phrase אֹרֶךְ הַיְרִיעָה הָאַחַת, which appears twice in פרשת תרומה (Exod 26,2. 8) and twice in פרשת ויקהל (Exod 36,9. 15) is probably the best illustration of this problematic issue, where two variables act simultaneously in opposing tendencies:[12]

Munaḥ-legarmeh appears twice in Exodus 26:

אָרֶךְו הירִיעָה האחֹת

In this case the accentuation was determined according, to the length of the division-word, since Munaḥ-Legarmeh is preferred in a short division-word stressed on the first syllable.

However, in Exodus 36 Geresh appears:

אֹרֶךְ הירִיעָה האחֹת

It is most probable that in this case, the accentuation was determined according to the characteristics of the part to the left of the division-place, for Geresh is preferred before long words.

The rabbinic scholars (חז"ל) observed these two ways of accentuation and said[13]:

כל אורך דצוא' במונח ודעשיה בגרש, וסימן דפקיד יתיב ודעביד קאים

This midrash serves as a mnemonic device, yet does not probe into the issue of differing accentuation. Such an ambivalent accentuation, as mentioned before, can be understood only in view of the notion that each pattern is characterized by a compound of interrelating variables.

---

12. A short word stressed on the first syllable - אֹרֶךְ, with two long words to its left - הירִיעָה האחת.

13. Miqra'ot Gedolot, Masora Parva (Exod 26,8).

In fact, we found six variables which affect the accentuation in Parallel Patterns. These are:

1. The status of the accent at the division-place (henceforth: divider), namely, existence or absence of additional subdivisions prior to the division-place.

2. The length of the words.

3. The number of words.

4. Linguistic criteria (syntactic or semantic).

5. The divisional structure in the section to the left of the division-place (namely, the location of an additional - potential or actual - subdivision, to the left of the division-place).

6. The location of the verse in the biblical corpus.

The accentuation in each and every Parallel Pattern is conditioned by several variables. Some variables of greater and some of lesser influence were noted. Organizing them in descending order of their effectiveness in each pattern, is essential for a whole and accurate description. This principle can be demonstrated in verses where a division - potential or actual - is adjacent to the Revia:

A conjunctive (Munaḥ) instead of disjunctive may come in a word adjacent to Revia, when there are only three words in the domain of the Revia:

וַיֹּאמֶר לָו / הֹ' (Gen 4,15).

The same may occur when there are four words or more in the domain of the Revia, as long as there is a division at the third word preceding the Revia (there are 8 exceptions):

בְּיוֹם הַהֹוּא // יִשָּׂא עֲלֵיכֶם / מָשָׁל (Micah 2,4).

Here there is a division at the third word before Revia, and the word adjacent to Revia has Munaḥ.

A statistical check of these verses in comparison with similar verses, in which Geresh comes at the adjacent word to Revia shows, that the usual accentuation at the division-place is by Geresh, while a conjunctive occurs only in 25% of the cases discussed.

We have discovered that the accentuation in these Parallel Patterns is conditioned by two variables:

1. The status of the divider.
2. The length of the two words preceding the Revia.

An examination of the verses according to the status of the divider reveals that where there is no prior division in the domain of Revia, Geresh comes in 86% of the cases:

ויֹּאמר לָהֶם / אלהֹים (Gen 1,28).

Where there is a prior division, the conjunctive is preferred in 64% of the cases (as is demonstrated in Micah 2,4 above). The statistical data are given in Table I below.

Table I:
Statisics for distribution according to the status of the divider

| Status of divider | Geresh | conjunctive | total |
|---|---|---|---|
| No prior division | 86% | 14% | 100% |
| Prior division | 36% | 64%(!) | 100% |
| Total | 75% | 25% | 100% |

An examination of the verses according to the length of words reveals that Geresh is increasingly used as the words preceding the Revia get longer: it appears in only 57% of the cases where the two words preceding the Revia are not long (see again Gen. 1,28).
Where only one of the words preceding the Revia is long, Geresh appears in 75% of the cases:

(2 Sam 21,14) [ויקברו את-עצמות-שאול ויהונתן-בנו] בָּאֶרֶץ בנימִֹן / בצלֹע.

Where both words preceding the Revia are long, Geresh appears in 86% of the cases :

(Ezek 42,5) כי-יוכֹלו אתיקים / מהֵֹנה.

Table II:
Statistics for distribution according to the length of the words

| Length of words | Geresh | conjunctive | total |
|---|---|---|---|
| No long words | 57% | 43% | 100% |
| Only one long word | 75% | 25% | 100% |
| Two long words | 86% | 14% | 100% |
| Total | 75% | 25% | 100% |

In view of these findings we see, that the intensity of the first variable (the status of the divider) is stronger than the intensity of the second (length of words), since no cases in which the conjunctive is preferred are to be found with the second variable. Therefore a first classification was made according to the first variable and a sub-classification according to the second.

In the cases of prior division in the domain of the Revia, this classification was essential for clarifying the accentuation by a conjunctive, as well as explaining the uncommon occurrences of Geresh. Indeed it was found that, where there is a prior divider in the domain of Revia, Geresh is preferred in 67% of the cases where both words preceding the Revia are long:

(Jos 3,10). והורש יוריש מִפְּנֵיכֶם // אֶת-הַכְּנַעֲנִי וְאֶת-הַחִתִּי / וְאֶת-הַחִוִּי

In contrast, a conjunctive occurs in 78% of the cases of prior division where only one of the words is long:

(Gen 38,11). וַיֹּאמֶר יְהוּדָה לְתָמָר כַּלָּתוֹ // שְׁבִי אַלְמָנָה / בֵית-אָבִיךְ

Where neither word is long, a conjunctive occurs in 92% of the cases of prior division:

(Ruth 1,1). וַיֵּלֶךְ אִישׁ // מִבֵּית לֶחֶם / יְהוּדָה

Table III:
Distribution according to the length of the words in cases of prior
division

| Length of words | Geresh | conjunctive | total |
|---|---|---|---|
| No long words | 8% | 92% | 100% |
| Only one long word | 22% | 78% | 100% |
| Two long words | 67%(!) | 33% | 100% |
| Total | 36% | 64% | 100% |

As for the cases of no prior division - this classification sheds
some light on the occurrences of uncommon accentuation by a conjunctive. It was found that such an accentuation is preferred (=67%),
where the Revia's word is not long, and both words preceding it are
short, stressed on the first syllable. For example:

שְׁלָשׁ מֵאוֹת / אַמָּה (Gen 6,15).

In all the other cases of no prior division Geresh is preferred.

To conclude

Our study has probed into the inner dynamic process of Parallel
Patterns distribution. We have traced repetitive formats, formulated
rules, and expounded some discrepancies in the verses. Still much is
yet to be done.

The description of each and every pattern highlights positions
where the distribution of accents in the verse is rather clear, as well as
positions of ambivalent accentuation.

Tracing the positions of clear distribution is essential to the formulation of rules, and there is no doubt that it constitutes the core of
this research. Yet identifying the ambivalent positions (where no conclusion may be reached) is not less important, for the existence of
ambivalent cases along with positions of clear distribution indicates the
gradual development of Parallel Patterns in the process of reading the
text, and comes to show the natural process of the formation of the
accentuation system.

## BIBLIOGRAPHY

Breuer 1982

מ' ברויאר, טעמי המקרא בכ"א ספרים ובספרי אמ"ת, ירושלים תשמ"ב.

Luzzatto 1852

ש"ד לוצטו, "אגרת נחמדה על אודות הטעמים", תורת אמת, י' בער [מחבר],
רדלהיים 1852 [ד"צ: ירושלים תשל"א].

Spanier 1927

A. Spanier, *Die massoretischen Akzente*, Berlin 1927.

Weil 1982

G. E. Weil et al., *Concordance de la cantilation de Premiers Prophètes*, éditions C.N.R.S., 1982.

Wickes 1881

W. Wickes, טעמי אמ"ת *A Treatise on the Accentuation of the three so-called Poetical Books of the Old Testament, Psalms, Proverbs and Job*, Oxford 1881 (repr.: New York 1970).

Wickes 1887

W. Wickes, טעמי כ"א ספרים *A Treatise on the Accentuation of the twenty-one so-called Prose Books of the Old Testament*, Oxford 1887 (repr.: New York 1970).

# A MASORETIC LIST OF BABYLONIAN ORIGIN OF DOTTED WORDS IN THE PENTATEUCH

Yosef Ofer
The Hebrew University of Jerusalem

## 1. Lists of Dotted Words

Many halakhic and masoretic literary sources list fifteen dotted words in the Bible, ten in the Pentateuch, four in the Prophets and a single word in the Hagiographa. These words appear in a Scroll of the Law with dots over some or all their letters. Midrashic literature drew various halakhic or aggadic conclusions from these dots. Scholars generally hold that the dots were added in order to note doubts or disagreements in the Biblical text. This opinion is already implied in Rabbinic sources.[1]

The subject of this paper is an ancient masoretic list in which some forty Pentateuchal verses appear, containing dotted words or let-

---

1. The list appears in *Sifre Bemidbar* 69 (ed. Horovitz, p. 64 ff.); *Avot deRabbi Nathan*, version a, ch. 34; version b, ch. 37 (ed. Schechter, pp. 97-101); *Tractate Soferim* 6, 3 (ed. Higger, pp. 166-169); S. Frensdorff, *Ochlah W'ochlah*, Hannover 1864, p. 96, list 99; and other sources. See: S. Lieberman, *Greek and Hellenism in Jewish Palestine* [Heb.], Jerusalem 1962, p. 182-184 (and note 42 there); C.D. Ginsburg, *Introduction to the Massoretico-Critical Edition of the Hebrew Bible*[2], New York 1966 (henceforth Ginsburg, *Introduction*), p. 318-333; I. Yeivin, *Introduction to the Tiberian Masorah*[4] [Heb.], Jerusalem 1983, p. 37-38.

ters. The ten dotted words in the common list do not appear in this list, which appears - with minor differences - in two sources. The one is a Tiberian manuscript of the Pentateuch (ms. Leningrad, Firkovitch B10, henceforth: L3), the list appearing in the masoretic inscriptions at the end of the manuscript.[2] The second source is a two-page Geniza fragment containing various masoretic notations[3] (henceforth: מס10). Before discussing the list, we must note that it was published some thirty years ago by F. Diaz-Esteban,[4] but he overlooked several basic points we shall discuss here.

Here is the full text of the list in both sources:

| Ms. מס10 (page 1, recto) | | Ms. L3[5] |
|---|---|---|
| אליין מלייה בקרייה דכתיבן לבר מן דפה | | אלין מלייא באורייתא דכתיבן לבד מן דפה ז' |
| ומנקדן מירום מלתה או מירום אתה ואינון זיטימה ומחלוקת ופליגין עליהון | | ומנקדין מירום מלתא או מירום אתא ואינון זיטימא ומחלוקת ופליגין עליהון |
| בראשית | | בראשית |
| את המאור הגדול | Gen 1,16 | 1. את המאור הגדל |
| ושם הנר השני | Gen 2,13 | 2. ושם הנהר השני גיחון |
| הוא הסובב תינינה | Gen 2,13 | 3. הוא הסובב תיני' |

---

2. This list was published by C.D. Ginsburg, *The Massorah compiled from Manuscripts*, III, London 1885 [henceforth: Ginsburg, *The Massorah*], p. 278.

3. Ms. Heb. d 62,7 of the Bodleian Library of Oxford. The fragment is numbered מס10 by: I. Yeivin, *The Hebrew Language Tradition as reflected in the Babylonian Vocalization* [Heb.], Jerusalem 1985, p. 206. Other manuscripts mentioned in this article and marked מסx are described by Yeivin there.

4. F. Díaz Esteban,"El Fragmento Babilónico Ms. Heb. d. 62 fol. 7 de la Bodleiana de Oxford", *Boletin de la Asociation Espanola de Orientalistas* 2 (1966), pp. 89-107; 3 (1967), p. 244.

5. Bold letters indicate the changes between the two sources. Underlined letters are dotted in the manuscript.

|  | | |
|---|---|---|
| Gen 4,3 | וַיְהִי מקץ ימים | ויהי מקץ ימים ויבא .4 |
| Gen 4,22 | את תובל קין | את תובל קין לטש כל .5 |
| Gen 4,22 | ואחות תובל קין | ואחות תובל קין נעמה .6 |
| Gen 8,17 | הוצא אתך | הוצא אתך ושרצו .7 |
| Gen 24,60 | אחתנו את היי | אחתינו את היי לאלפי .8 |
| Gen 26,32 | ויגדו לו על אדות | ויגדו לו על אדות הבאר .9 |
| Gen 27,3 | וצודה לי צידה | וצודה לי צידה .10 |
| Gen 37,36 | לפוטיפר סריס | לפוטיפר סריס פרעה .11 |
| Gen 39,1 | ויקנהו פוטיפר | ויקנהו פוטיפר סריס .12 |
| Gen 39,20 | אשר אסורי המ' | אשר אסורי המלך .13 |
| Gen 41,45?, 50?; Gen 46,20 | בת פוטי פרע | בת פוטיפרע כהן .14 |
| Gen 46,13 | תולע ופוה ויוב / ואלה שמות | תולע ופוה ויוב ושמרן / ואלה שמות .15 |
| Ex 6,25 | לקח לו מבנות פוטיאל | מבנות פוטיאל לו לאשה .16 |
| Ex 16,2 | וילינו כל עדת בני | וילונו כל עדת בני ישראל .17 |
| Ex 16,6 | כי תלונו עלינו | כי תלונו עלינו סוף פסוק .18 |
| Ex 17,4 | עוד מעט וסקלני | עוד מעט וסקלני .19 |
| Ex 17,6 | על כסיה מלחמה | ויאמר כי יד על כס יה .20 |
| Ex 23,26 | לא תהיה משכלה | לא תהיה משכלה ועקרה .21 |
| Ex 40,22 | ויתן את השלחן / ויקרא | ———— .22 / ויקרא |
| Lev 5,14 | וַיְד' יי דנפש כי תמעל | וידבר דנפש כי תחטא [!] Lv 4,1 .23 |
| Lev 14,21 | ואם דל הוא ואין | ואם דל הוא ואין ידו משגת .24 |
| Lev 21,5 | לא יקרחה קרחה | לא יקרחה ‹קר'› בראשם ופאת .25 |
| Lev 26,18 | ואם עד אלה / וידבר | ואם עד אלה לא תשמעו .26 / וידבר |
| Num 1,6 | אלה קריאי העדה | אלה קרואי העדה נשיאי .27 |
| Num 13,32 | ויציאו דבת הארץ | ויציאו דבת הארץ .28 |
| Num 16,11 | כי תלונו עלינו | כי תלונו עליו [!] .29 |
| Num 22,5 | הנה כסה | הנה כסה את ע' .30 |
| Num 24,23 | משמו אל | מי יחיה משמו אל .31 |
| Num 27,11 | לשארו הקרב אליו | לשארו הקרב אליו .32 |
| Num 29,26 | וביום החמישי | וביום החמישי פרים .33 |
| Num 32,7 | ולמה תנואון / אלה הדברים | ולמה תניאון את לב .34 / אלה הדברים |

| | | | |
|---|---|---|---|
| Deut 2,8 | וַנֵּפֶן וַנַּעֲבֹר | וַנֵּפֶן וַנַּעֲבֹר דרך הבשן [!] Dt 3,1 | ונפן ונעבר דרך הבשן .35 |
| Deut 4,37 | ויוצאך בפניו | ויוצאך בפניו בכחו .36 |
| Deut 4,43 | ואת ראמת בגלעד | ואת ראמת בגלעד .37 |
| Deut 5,9 | ולשמרי מצותו | ולשמרי מצותו .38 |
| Deut 22,20 | ואם אמת היה | ואם אמת היה הדבר .39 |
| Deut 31,7 | כי אתה תבוא | כי אתה תבא את העם .40 |
| Deut 31,9 | ויכתב משה | ויכתב משה את הדברים .41 |
| | אלו הדברים ביני מערביא וביני | |
| | מדנחיא בתורה | |

## 2. The Title of the List and its Conclusion

Let us first examine the title of the list (as it appears in מס100):

אליין מלייה בקרייה דכתיבן לבר מן דפה
ומנקדן מירום מלתה או מירום אתה
ואינון זיטימה ומחלוקת ופליגין עליהון

The first line talks about writing outside the page. What does this mean? From the wording of the second source we learn that a sign resembling a final *nun* is inscribed in the margins of the page. Such a sign appears in Tiberian and Babylonian manuscripts to denote cases of *qere* and *kethiv* - and so it would seem that here, too, it denotes some sort of problem in the Biblical text. Yeivin (Yeivin, *Introduction*, p. 44) proposes to view the symbol as an abbreviation of the word זיטימה, (derived from a Greek word meaning "baseness" or "error"), which appears in the third and last line of the title.

The title goes on to mention the dots that the masorah would have marked above the doubtful words or letters, while from the last line we learn that this symbol indicates "disagreement". To explain the meaning of the dots, the masorah adduces three expressions in three different languages: זיטימה in Greek, מחלוקת in Hebrew, and פליגין עליהון in Aramaic.

The last line of the list seems to be its conclusion: אלו הדברים ביני מערביא וביני מדנחיא בתורה. Various scholars have deduced from this sentence that the list of dotted words is one of disagreements between Palestinian and Babylonian Jews. Yet, there seems to us to be a difficulty in this explanation - for a number of reasons: first of all, the list has been defined at length in its title - and what reason can there be for additional explanation at the end? Secondly, there would seem to be some opposition, or even a contradiction, between the opening and the conclusion. The opening speaks generally of dots and disagreement, whereas the conclusion talks of easterners and westerners. Thirdly, the wording of the conclusion appears in only one of the two sources of the lists (in ממס10), but is missing in the other source (L3). In ממס10 there appears a certain graphic sign, something like two circles joined by an arc, between the list and its conclusion. This symbol would seem to be one denoting separation, showing that the masorah is at this point going on to something new. This is its meaning when it appears a few times on the second page of the fragment. This second page of the Geniza fragment was discovered by Yeivin, who joined it to the first page published earlier by Díaz-Esteban.

All these considerations lead to the conclusion that there is no connection between the last line on the page and the list we are considering here. We shall yet try to demonstrate the validity of this conclusion by a consideration of the material itself.

## 3. Disagreements marked by the dots

What are the disagreements marked by the dots? Out of a comparison with other masoretic sources - especially those of the Babylonian masorah - it is possible to assume with full certainty just what the disagreement implied is. In the appendix I have listed the various kinds of disagreement, and I have adduced evidence in support of my assumption wherever such evidence was available to me.

All the dots denote disagreements in the Biblical text, not in the way the text is to be read. This is why the linguistic differences between the Tiberian and Babylonian language traditions are not reflected in them, for almost all of these differences are connected with the way the words are to be read, rather than the way they are to be written.

Some of the dots denote disagreements in the way the text is to be divided up, a field almost completely overlooked by the Tiberian masorah. Many of these disagreements are to be found in the list of disagreements of the scholars of Nehardea - in Geniza manuscript 510מ.

Other topics of disagreement include writing as one word or as two, a case of **qere** and **kethiv**, the use of **waw conjunctiva** and **plene** or **defectiva** spellings. The number of cases in every topic is given in the following table:

| Sort of disagreement | number of cases | evidence of disagreement |
|---|---|---|
| A. open and closed portions | 10 | 7 |
| B. writing as one word or as two | 8 | 5 |
| C. *qere* and *kethiv* | 11 | 7 |
| D. plene or defectiva spellings | 7 | 1 |
| E. *waw conjunctiva* | 2 | - |
| F. doubtful cases and others | 3 | - |
| **Total** | **41** | **20** |

### 4. The Babylonian origin of the list

The summarizing table shows that twenty of the forty disagreements are clearly supported in Babylonian masorah sources. Almost everywhere it can be seen that the disagreement is an internal one, within the Babylonian masorah, and not a disagreement between Babylon and Tiberias. In fact, our claim is a two-fold one: the disagreements indicated by the dots are internal Babylonian disagreements, and furthermore, the very tradition of denoting doubt by means of dots in various places is of Babylonian origin. Let us sum up the evidence as follows:

Firstly, we have seen that in half the cases there is clear evidence of an internal Babylonian disagreement.[6]

---

6. In some cases, we also find evidence of a disagreement between Palestine and Babylon, but it must be remarked that every internal Babylonian disagreement can also be seen as a disagreement between Palestine and Babylon. Let us assume that there existed a disagreement between two Babylonian schools of thought, such as between Sura and Nehardea, while in Palestine only one of these opinions had

Secondly, we have already seen that one topic of disagreement is the way certain open or closed Pentateuch paragraphs are to be written. The very consideration of these open or closed paragraphs is an integral part of the Babylonian masorah, and the only paragraph lists known to us are of Babylonian origin. On the other hand, the Tiberian masorah does not deal at all with open and closed paragraphs, and the tradition of writing these paragraphs in manuscripts was not uniform. It is thus difficult to assume that this masorah includes a way of marking places of disagreement on this topic.

The third piece of evidence relates to the tradition of using dots to mark these places. In Tiberian manuscripts and in other places in the Tiberian masorah there is no sign of dotted words other than the fifteen known examples. In contrast, the Babylonian masorah indicates a number of dotted words, including two within our list (פוטיפרע and תנואון).[7]

If this is so, then an important question arises: the list we are discussing appears in two manuscripts, one Tiberian (L3) and the other semi-Tiberian (מס100).[8] If the origin of the list is Babylonian, how did it come to appear in Tiberian manuscripts? In my opinion, there is

---

any support: the Palestinian masoretes can say that there is a difference of opinion between the Palestinian version and that of a certain school in Babylon, but - in our opinion - these disagreements originate in Babylon, which is where the custom developed to dot doubtful words.

7. Both words are mentioned in the Babylonian masorah to Gen 16,5 (Ms. מס90): יוד דפוטיפרע דויולד נקוד עליו ופלגי... תניאון דכת׳ תנואון נקוד על וא קדם׳ ופלוג׳. The dotted word פוטיפרע (Gen 46,20) is also mentioned in the masorah parva of Ms. למ there (See: M. Breuer, *The Masorah Magna to the Pentateuch by Shemuel ben Ya'aqov [Ms. למ]*, New York 1992, p. 5). The dotted word תנואון (Num 32,7) is also mentioned in the Babylonian masorah there (Ms. מס110; Ginsburg, *The Massorah*, III, p. 238).

8. The manuscript has Babylonian vocalization symbols and Tiberian symbols as well. See: Yeivin (above, note 3).

nothing unusual about such a phenomenon. In my doctoral dissertation[9] I have pointed out the existence of a broad process whereby the Babylonian masorah influenced its Tiberian counterpart. It is difficult to find an ancient Tiberian manuscript free of such influence: even the most clearly Tiberian manuscript - the Aleppo Codex - shows signs of Babylonian influence in a number of places. The Tiberian masorah tended naturally to absorb external material, for it had no fixed order, each masorete creating his own masoretic collection which he would then record in the margins of his page.

## 5. An acrostichonic signature in Geniza fragment מס10

Let us now consider an interesting feature further along in Geniza fragment מס10: on the obverse side of the page, there appear many masoretic lists written in smaller letters, most of which are of the accumulative masorah type. In one of these lists there appears a clearly acrostichonic signature: שעיד בן כדרוי חזק

| | | | |
|---|---|---|---|
| Lam 1,1 | - | ל' | שָׁרְתִּי |
| Lam 3,59 | - | ל' | עַוָּתָתִי |
| Jer 50,24 | - | ל' | יָקֹשְׁתִּי |
| Deut 9,24 | - | ל' | דַּעְתִּי |
| | | | |
| Esth 5,8 | - | ל' | בַּקָּשָׁתִי |
| Ps 139,15 | - | ל' | רֻקַּמְתִּי |
| | | | |
| Gen 50,5 | - | ל' | כָּרִיתִי |
| Ps 142,7[10] | - | ל' בטע' | דַּלּוֹתִי |
| 2 Kgs 2,21 | - | [ל'] | רִפִּיתִי |

---

9. Y. Ofer, *The Babylonian Masorah of the Pentateuch, its Principles and Methods*, Thesis submitted for the Degree Doctor of Philosophy to the Senate of the Hebrew University, Jerusalem 1995. See especially chapter 14 there.

10. It is possible that the masorah refers to Ps 116, 6, which is the single time in the Bible that the word דַּלּוֹתִי is stressed on its last syllable.

| | | | |
|---|---|---|---|
| Ex 23,27 | – | ל' | וְהַמֹּתִי |
| Gen 31,51 | – | ל' | יָרִיתִי |
| | | | |
| Cant 2,3 | – | ל' | חִמַּדְתִּי |
| Job 32,6 | – | ל' | זָחַלְתִּי |
| Gen 9,13 | – | ל' | קַשְׁתִּי |

The list adduces *hapax legomena* ending in -תִי. It can be seen that when the masorete reached the letter *daleth* for the second time, he found no suitable *hapax legomenon*, and so he adduced a word appearing only once in its stress pattern (a penultimate or ultimate stressed syllable).

To denote the letter *samekh* in the name סעיד a biblical word beginning in a *sin* is adduced (שׂרתי). Such a custom can be found in poetic acrostichons (like שמחים בצאתם in the poem אל אדון recited in the morning prayer on Shabbat [Saturday]), as well as in scores of alphabetic lists in the Ochlah W'Ochlah collection.[11]

The name סעיד בן כדרוי is unknown in any other source. The name סעיד became very common after the Arab conquest, but the name כדרוי is unique and is not known from any other source. In the Babylonian Talmud (Yoma 60b) the name כידור is mentioned and is interpreted negatively. The root meaning in Arabic is also linked with ugliness and sadness. The suffix of the name כדרוי is unusual, and seems to denote to some degree the time and place of the owner of the name. The suffix -oy is of Persian origin, and names ending in this suffix were common in the eighth and ninth centuries, especially in Babylon. Amongst the geonim we find in Sura such names as **Biboi** (served in 776) and **Qimoi** (824), while in Pumpedita there appear such names as **Natroi** (752), **Shinoi** (781), **Paltoi** (842) and **Qimoi** (897). **Parqoi ben Baboi** is the disciple of Rav Yehudai Gaon. The scribe of the yeshiva of Rav Zemah bar **Paltoi** was named **Mishoi**. Additional names of this type are **Isqoi** (= יצחק), **Bradoi** and **Bakhtoi**.[12]

---

11. E.g. Ochlah W'ochlah (above, note 1), lists 1, 6, 7, 8, 9, 13.

12. See: N. Allony, "An Autograph of Saʿid ben Farjoi of the ninth Century", *Textus* 6 (1968), pp. 109; S. Havlin, "Torat Ha-Ge'onim u-Tqufatam" in: *Toratam Shel Ge'onim*, Jerusalem 1993 [Heb.], pp. 31-42.

It is interesting to note that the name which arises from our acrostichon is very similar to a name mentioned in a biblical manuscript of the Pentateuch (לו, Chufut Kale 36, Leningrad Firkovitch B17). This Ms. was written by Shelomo Halevi bar Boyaʿa, who wrote also the Aleppo Codex. He siged his name: שלמה הלוי בר בויאעא תלמיד סעיד בן פרגוי המכונה בלקוק (Shelomo HaLevi the son of Boyaʿa, a pupil of Said ben Pargoi known as Balquq [or Alquq]).[13] This name apparently appears in a fragmented colophon published by Aloni.[14]

Was this acrostrichon written by the scribe of ms. מסׁ10 ? Or perhaps he copied it from another masorah page? We shall try to answer this question on the basis of the nature of the other masorah lists appearing in the manuscript.

The second page of מסׁ10 - identified by Yeivin - is very significant. The masoretic material in this page (on both sides) is far more plentiful than that which was inscribed at the end of the first page, thus enabling us better to appreciate its substance. There appear masoretic notes, most of which are comments of an accumulative masorah made up of *hapax legomena*. The words in each list have the same initial or final letters.

As far as these masoretic comments are concerned, they would seem to be organized in the same order as the Biblical text. The first word in each list (and rarely another word in the list) match this order. On the two pages there appear 31 masoretic lists, and only two of these are unlike the Biblical order.

In light of this data, I should like to make a proposal, concerning the way this collection of masoretic comments came about in this manuscript: some masorete collected up notes from the masorah magna of

---

13. See: S. Baer und H.L. Strack. *Die Dikduke Ha-Tᵉamim des Ahron ben Moscheh ben Ascher*, Leipzig 1879. pp. xxxvi-xxxvii; P. Kahle, *Masoreten des Westens*, Stuttgart 1927, pp. 58-59; I. Yeivin, *The Aleppo codex of the Bible*, Jerusalem 1968 [henceforth: Yeivin, *The Aleppo Codex*], pp. 366-367

14. N. Allony (above, note 12), pp. 106-117.

some Tiberian masorah manuscript. The masorete generally selected notes of an accumulative masorah, and it may well be that he was looking specifically for a masorah written in a special ornamental fashion, as was customary with accumulative masorah. In this way we can also explain the distribution of the notes - one or two notes per chapter, with entire chapters overlooked.

The acrostichonic list appears within these masoretic lists without any special mark, and it would seem that the person who collected up the masoretic lists is not the one who composed the acrostichonic signature. This would seem to have the creation of the masorete who processed the biblical page from which a scribe copied over the manuscript. The latter copied over the note without noticing its special character.

This is the second time an acrostichonic signature has come up in lists of accumulative masorah, and it joins the signature of the masorete appearing three times in the British Museum manuscript Or. 4445: נִיסִי בֶּן דָּנִיֵּאל הַכֹּהֵן יִשְׁמְרֵהוּ אֵל (Nisi son of Daniel the kohen, may God guard him). Lyons and Dotan identified this signature separately.[15] However, whereas in that case there is no doubt that the masorete of the manuscript is the same one who formulated the note and introduced his name into it, in our case it would seem that the manuscript copyist had no idea at all that there was an acrostichonic signature in the material he was copying over.

15. D. Lyons. "An Acrostichonic Signature in the Masorah Lists", *Qiryat Sefer* 61 (1987), pp. 141-145 [Heb.]; A. Dotan, "Reflections Towards a Critical Edition of Pentateuch Codex Or. 4445", *Estudios Masoréticos* (X Congreso de la IOMS), Madrid 1993, pp. 39-51.

**Appendix: Sorting of the Dotted Words according to kinds of disagreements**

## A. open and closed portions

2. ‏וַשֵם הנהר השני‏ - Gen 2,13

   מס510: The verse is included in a list of closed portions on which the scribes of Neharde‘a have another opinion (‏"פליגין עליהון סיפרי נהרדעאי"‏)

4. ‏וַיְהִי מקץ ימים‏ - Gen 4,3

   מס510: The verse is included in a list of closed portions on which the scribes of Neharde‘a have another opinion.

21. ‏לא תהיה משכלה‏ - Ex 23,26

    מס510: The verse is included in a list of closed portions on which the scribes of Neharde‘a have another opinion; מס100: ‏פ‏"ר (no portion); The accepted text [Henceforth: T]: closed portion: Ms. Leningrad B19a [Henceforth: L]: no portion.

22. ‏ויתן את השלחן‏ - Ex 40,22

23. ‏וַיד' יי דנפש כי תמעל‏ - Lev 5,14

24. ‏ואם דל הוא ואין‏ - Lev 14,21

    מס510: The verse is included in a list of closed portions on which the scribes of Neharde‘a have another opinion.

    A list of portions from the Geniza (Westminster College, Misc. 4,65-66): ‏<סת' ופולג' ופי אלספר ליס הו פצל ‏‏ובכט סת'>‏ [ = a closed portion, and there is a difference of opinion about that. (In arabic:) no portion in 'the book', and a closed portion in 'the manuscript'].

26. ‏ואם עד אלה‏ - Lev 26,18

    T: no portion; מס510: The verse is not included in the list of closed portions; Two lists of portions from the Geniza (Cambridge T-S D1,87, Westminster College, Misc. 4, 65-66) and L: closed portion

35. ‏וַנפן ונעבר‏ - Deut 2,8

    מס110 Deut 2,8: ‏ונפן ונעבר סת' ופול' ולא ר‏‏"פ הוא.‏

39. ‏ואם אמת היה‏ - Deut 22,20

41. ‏וַיכתב משה‏ - Deut 31,9

    מס510: The verse is included in a list of closed portions on which the scribes of Neharde‘a have another opinion (The order of the verses there proves that the verse under discussion is verse 9 and not verse 22).

**B. writing as one word or as two words**

5. את תובל קין - Gen 4,22

6. ואחות תובל קין - Gen 4,22

masorah magna of *Miqra'ot Gedolot* (Venice 1524), Gen 46,20:

"תובל קין למדינחאי מילתא חדא כתב וקריין למערבאי תרין מלין כתיב וקרין";

See also Ms Vienna 13 and Ginsburg Bible, to Gen 46,20; C.D. Ginsburg, *Introduction*, p. 200.

11. לפוטיפר סריס - Gen 37,36

12. ויקנהו פוטיפר - Gen 39,1

14. בת פוטי פרע - Gen 41,45?, 50?; 46,20?

Ms 9 מסס Gen 16, 5: יוד דפוטיפָרָע דויולד נקוד עליו ופלגי (= Gen 46,20).

Ms מל Gen 46,20, masorah parva (Breuer, p. 5): יוד דפוטיפר' נקוד ופולג'.

*Liqqute Qadmoniyyot* (ed. Pinsker, Wien 1860, p. ל, on Gen 41, 45): זה מחלפין בו בת פוטיפרע חדא מלתא כתבין וכן מתנקד. וי"א בת פוטי פרע כתבין תרתין מלין וננקד כן תרתין מלין. See I. Ben David, *Leshonenu* 56 [1991], p. 129; Yeivin, *The Aleppo Codex*, p. 83.

The first two sources indicate Gen 46,20 as the dotted word, while according to the third source the disagreement is about Gen 41,45.

20. על כסיה מלחמה - Ex 17, 16

Ms מל Ex 17,16:[כסיה =] כעיה אמרין ומע'... כסיה.

Ms שו Ex 17, 16: ל' וחד מלה למע'

Ms 7 מס (p. 3r.): כתי' בתרי נהרדעי ובסיפרי כתי בחד דסוראי בסיפרי... כסיה.

See: Yeivin, *Aleppo codex*, p. 82.

31. משמו אל - Num 24,73

Ms 7 מס (p. 3r): משמו לחוד וקודשא לחוד משמו כתי' נהרדעי בחד כתי' סוראי – משמואל לחוד.

16.? לקח לו מבנות פוטיאל - Ex 6, 25

**C. *Qere* and *Kethiv***

7. הוצא אתך - Gen 8,17

Ms 11 מסס ופולג': כת' הוצא היצא

10. וצודה לי צידה - Gen 27,3

Ginsburg, *The Masorah*, list 34ה; Ochlah W'Ochlah (ed. Frensdorff, 1864), list 112: פלוגתא דרב נחמן

13. אשר אסורי המ' - Gen 39,20

17. Ex 16,2 - וַיִּלּוֹנוּ כל עדת בני

Ms למ Ex 16,2: וילונו במדבר וילינו כת׳ ופלוג׳ (a fragmentary remark appears also in ms 2סמ there).

18. Ex 16,7 - כי תלונו עלינו

Ms 2סמ Ex 16,7: תלינו ב׳ דק] ונחנו מה פולג׳.

19. Ex 17,4 - עוד מעט וסקלני

Ms 1סמ: וסקלוני דק וסקלני כת׳[16]

Meir Abul'afya (רמ״ה), *Masoret Seyag la-Tora*, Firence 1750, root סקל (p. 47b): עוד מעט וסקלני׳ – חסר וי״ו כתיב יו״ד בתר נו״ן וכן קרי. ולסוראי וסקלנו כתיב וי״ו בסוף תיבותא וקרי יו״ד. וליתה דכלהי נוסחי דיקי יו״ד כתיב ויו״ד קרי. ובמחזורא רבא[17] חד מן אלפא ביתא דכתב׳ ו :619חַ Ginsburg, *The Massorah*, list וקור׳ יוד. וסקלני ל׳ מנהון והוא פלוגתא בין סורא לנהרדעי.

25. Lev 21,5 - לא יקרחה קרחה

27. Num 1,16 - אלה קריאי העדה

Ms 11סמ Num 1,16: קרואי קדמ׳ דק קריאי כת׳ ופלוג׳

29. Num 16,11 - כי תלֹנו עליו

34. Num 32,7 - ולמה תנואון

Ms 11סמ Num 32,7: תניאון דק תנואון כת׳ ונקוד על וא קדמ׳.

Ms 9סמ Gen 16,5: תניאון דכת׳ תנואון נקוד על וא קדמ׳ ופולג׳.

See: Ginsburg, *The Masorah*, list 620חַ; Ginsburg, *Introduction*, p. 206.

38. Deut 5, 9 - ולשמרי מצותַו

## D. Plene or Defectiva spellings

1. Gen 1,16 - את המאור הגדֹול

Ms למ Gen 1,16: הגדול ט׳ מל׳ באור׳... המאור הגדול פולג׳ דסיר׳

The masorah magna of ש (Ms. Sasoon 507; now: Jerusalem Heb. 24° 5702) and the masorah magna of 1ש (Ms. Sasoon 1053) to Deut 34,12 say that there is a disagreement between the masoretes of Neharde'a (who write הגדול) and those of Sura (who write הגדל).

3. Gen 2,13 - הוא הסֹובב תינינה

---

16. The word כת׳ (instead of חס׳) may hint that according to some opinion there is a case of *Qere* and *Kethiv* here.

17. Read probably רבתא במסורתא. The masorah refers to Ochlah W'Ochlah (ed. Frensdorff, list 136).

8. אֹחָתֵנוּ את היי - Gen 24,60
9. וַיַּגִּדוּ לו על אדות - Gen 26,32
28. וַיֹּצִיאוּ דבת הארץ - Num 13,32
36. וַיּוֹצִאֲךָ בפניו - Deut 4,37
*37 ואת ראֵמֹת בגלעד - Deut 4,43

## E. *Waw conjunctiva*

30. הִנֵּה כסה - Num 22,5

MS 110מס Ex 32,34: This verse is included in a list of four verses which are written in corrected books (בסיפ' מוג''"). In all three verses a man can read by mistake וְהִנֵּה instead of הִנֵּה.

33? וּבַיּוֹם החמישי - Num 29,26[18]

## F. Doubtful cases and others

15. תולע ופוֻה ויוב - Gen 46,13[19]
32. לשארֹן הקרב אליו - Num 27,11.
40. כי אתה תבוֹא - Deut 31,7

---

18. Compare Num 29,35 (ביום השמיני, without *waw*). It is also possible that the disagreement is about closed or open portion.

19. The disagreement is probably about *waw conjunctiva* in the word ויוב. See the parallel list in 1 Chron 7,1: "ולבני יששכר תולע ופואה ישיב ושמרון ארבעה".

# LA SECONDE PARTIE DU *SEFER ʾOKLAH WEʾOKLAH*

Bruno Ognibeni
Université de Fribourg (Suisse)

Je vous présente aujourd'hui mon édition de la seconde partie du *sefer ʾoklah weʾoklah*, qui paraîtra dans la collection "Textos y Estudios Cardenal Cisneros", publiée par l'Instituto de Filología del Consejo Superior de Investigaciones Científicas de Madrid.

Le *sefer ʾoklah weʾoklah* a déjà été édité trois fois. En 1864 à Hanovre paraissait *Das Buch Ochlah W'Ochlah (Massora). Herausgegeben, übersetzt und mit erläuternden Anmerkungen versehen nach einer, soweit bekannt, einzigen, in der Kaiserlichen Bibliothek zu Paris befindlichen Handschrift von Dr. S. Frensdorff*. Le livre a été réédité anastatiquement à New York en 1972, par Ktav. Il contient une transcription complète du manuscrit de la Bibliothèque Nationale de Paris, hébr. 148. Comme il manquait d'un index des versets bibliques, je l'ai composé moi-même.[1]

Le manuscrit de Paris a été édité aussi en facsimilé, par D. S. Löwinger: *The Masora Magna to the Bible. Ochla ve-Ochla, Codex Paris*, Jérusalem 1978. La qualité de la reproduction n'est pas malheureusement excellente, et il y manque en outre deux pages (ff. 47 *verso* et 63 *verso*).

---

1. *Index biblique à la Ochlah w'Ochlah de S. Frensdorff*, Turin 1992 (Quaderni di Henoch 5).

Frensdorff ignorait qu'il y avait un autre manuscrit de la '*oklah* *we'oklah*, dans la Universitätsbibliothek de Halle (cote Y b Qu. 10). Ce fut H. Hupfeld qui en informa le monde scientifique, dans un article paru dans la *Zeitschrift der Deutschen morgenländischen Gesellschaft*,[2] où il offrait un résumé assez détaillé de son contenu et une comparaison avec le manuscrit de Paris. Ch. D. Ginsburg déclara emphatiquement: "It is therefore of the utmost importance that the Halle MS. should be published... it will be a burning shame if those who love the Bible, and are anxious for a correct text of the Old Testament verity, do not come in aid in the publication of the newly discovered MS".[3] Hélas, il fallut attendre plus qu'un siècle pour voir l'édition que Ginsburg souhaitait avec tant d'ardeur.

Elle fut enfin réalisée par F. Díaz Esteban: *Sefer 'Oklah we-'Oklah. Colección de listas de palabras destinadas a conservar la integridad del texto hebreo de la Biblia entre los judíos de la Edad Media*, Madrid 1975 (Textos y Estudios 4). Elle contient la transcription de la première partie du manuscrit de Halle, avec un apparat de variantes en bas de page. Les variantes sont tirées de l'édition de Frensdorff et d'un certain nombre de manuscrits fragmentaires, découverts en 1926 par P. Kahle dans la 2me collection Firkovic à St. Pétersbourg et en 1954 par Díaz Esteban lui-même dans les fonds de la Genizah conservés à Oxford et Cambridge.

Díaz Esteban n'édita que la première partie du manuscrit de Halle, c'est-à-dire les ff. (4)-67.[4] La seconde partie (qui dans le manus-

---

2. "Ueber eine bisher unbekannt gebliebene Handschrift der Masorah" *ZDMG* 21 (1867) 201-220.

3. *Jacob ben Chajim Ibn Adoniyah's Introduction to the Rabbinic Bible, Hebrew and English; with Explanatory Notes*, Londres 1867[2], 34-35.

4. Les ff. 5-6 ont été insérées à la mauvaise place par le relieur. La f. 4 est donc la sixième dans la succession correcte. Relevons encore que les ff. 7-8 et 21-22 ne sont pas originales, mais insérées successivement pour remplacer des feuilles perdues ou abimées.

crit porte le titre סדרא אחרינא) couvre les ff. 68-125. Elle contient 343 listes massorétiques, selon la numérotation du manuscrit: mais beaucoup d'entre elles sont des ensembles de listes, aussi le total dépasse nettement 700. Les versets bibliques enregistrés en elles sont environ 5900.

## Le *sefer ʾoklah weʾoklah*: une ou deux parties ?

Selon Díaz Esteban, ce סדרא אחרינא ne fait pas partie de la collection *ʾoklah weʾoklah* proprement dite. Ce serait un ajout postérieur,[5] une sorte de *Erweiterungsschrift*. Ce jugement ne me paraît pas fondé. Voyons les faits suivants.

1) Dans le manuscrit de Halle à la f. 67 *verso* nous trouvons une prière, où le copiste remercie le Seigneur pour avoir terminé le סדר ראשני, et lui demande son aide pour commencer le ערך שני. Donc pour lui le livre qu'il copiait consistait d'une première et d'une seconde partie.

2) La table des matières au début du manuscrit (ff. 1-3 et 5-6) énumère soit les listes de la première partie soit de la seconde.

3) A la f. 124 *verso* nous trouvons une liste de dix-sept *simanin dilugim*, c'est-à-dire incomplets. Il s'agit de mots-clé dont on avait perdu la référence biblique: or treize d'entr'eux se rencontrent dans la première partie de la collection et quatre dans la seconde.

4) A la f. 78 *verso* nous lisons: דברך יׄגׄ חסרין וׄהׄ מלאין והם כתיבין דְּבָרֶיךָ", בסדרא קדמאה, 13 défectifs et 5 [faute pour 8] pleins, et ils sont déjà écrits dans la première partie". Les *simanin* ne sont pas écrits parce qu'ils l'ont déjà été dans la première partie de la collection: nous les trouvons en effet dans les §§ 114 et 115 de Díaz Esteban. En forme plus courte, c'est-à-dire avec le seul mot כתיבין "déjà écrits", on rencontre dans la seconde partie de la collection une vingtaine d'autres renvois à la première partie.

5) Le plus grand des manuscrits fragmentaires, Firkovic Ebr. II B 1554, renferme dans ses 18 feuilles environ 120 listes, 60 de la

---

5. "Añadidos posteriores" (*Sefer ʾOklah we-ʾOklah*, LXIII).

première partie du manuscrit de Halle et 60 de la seconde partie, dans la même succession.

6) Dans les marges d'un Pentateuque conservé a Lipsie,[6] le copiste (un certain Makir) cite à plusieurs reprises[7] la *masoret haggedola* de R. Gershom de Mayence et celle de R. Menahem de Joigny. Il s'agit sans doute de copies de la *'oklah we'oklah*.[8] Relevons la citation en marge de Nb 32,24, où Makir fait mention de la liste des 16. mots qui font sortir la lettre *alef*, donnant aussi son numéro: בסימן קֹמֹב מסידרא אחרי, "dans le signe 142 de la seconde partie". Makir connaissait donc un *sefer 'oklah we'oklah* composé de deux parties, comme celui du manuscrit de Halle.[9]

7) R. David Qimhi cite deux fois le *sefer 'oklah we'oklah* dans sa grammaire: la première fois[10] concernant שׁוּבָה *millera'*, la seconde[11] concernant גְבָל avec *pattah* et גְּבָל avec *qamaz*. Or nous pouvons constater que les שׁוּבָה *millera'* sont catalogués dans la seconde partie du manuscrit de Halle (§ 3 N de mon édition), alors que les גְּבָל/גְּבָל le sont dans la première partie (§ 24 de Díaz Esteban). Radaq cite donc

---

6. Universitätsbibliothek, BH1. C'est le n° 600 de la collation de Kennicott. Il a été copié en France vers la fin du XIIIme siècle.

7. En marge de Gn 40,2; 40,10; 50,25; Ex 14,26; 15,18; 28,30; Nb 32,24. Je n'ai pas vu directement le manuscrit, mais les transcriptions de P. J. Bruns, "De variis lectionibus Bibliorum Kennicottianarum", *RMBL* 12 (1783) 266. 269. 271. 276; 13 (1783), 53.

8. Sur les gloses de Makir s'appuyait H. Graetz pour affirmer que R. Gershom était l'auteur de la *'oklah we-'oklah*: "Der Autor des masoretischen Werkes Ochlah w'Ochlah", *MGWJ* 36 (1887) 1-34; "Ueber R. Gerschon und sein Verhältniß zum masoretischen Sammelwerk Ochlah W'Ochlah", *ibid.* 297-309. La thèse de Graetz ne tient pas debout: R. Gershom n'est sans doute pas l'auteur de la *'oklah*, mais probablement celui qui l'a fait connaître en Occident.

9. Dans le manuscrit de Halle cette liste porte le n° 152 de la seconde partie. Il faudrait contrôler le chiffre dans le manuscrit de Lipsie: Bruns peut bien avoir commis une faute de transcription.

10. *Sefer miklol*, ed. Rittenberg, Lyck 1862, 101b.

11. *Sefer miklol*, 146 a.

avec le nom de *sefer ʾoklah weʾoklah* des listes soit de la première soit de la seconde partie de la collection.

Tous ces faits démontrent que la seconde partie du manuscrit de Halle peut et doit être considérée comme faisant partie de l'oeuvre connue comme *ʾoklah weʾoklah*. C'est en effet un titre traditionnel et par conséquent les critères ne peuvent être que traditionnels. La collection s'est formée et développée progressivement, sans suivre une logique compositive interne.[12] On ne peut donc dire: "ceci est *ʾoklah*" ou "cela n'est pas *ʾoklah*", si ce n'est sur la base de la tradition. Est *ʾoklah* ce qui a été appelé *ʾoklah* de la part de témoins qualifiés. Si Radaq donne le nom d'*ʾoklah* à des listes de la première comme de la seconde partie du manuscrit de Halle, c'est une base suffisante pour que nous fassions la même chose.

On peut toutefois se demander pourquoi la collection se divise-t-elle en deux parties. La réponse ne peut être évidemment qu'hypothétique. Je propose l'explication suivante: la première partie s'intéresse plutôt aux consonnes,[13] la seconde plutôt au voyelles.[14] Si l'on considère que la tâche du massorète était d'un côté de corriger le texte consonantique copié par le *sofer* et de l'autre de le ponctuer, on ne trouvera pas illogique une organisation de la collection selon ces deux grandes lignes directrices.

Ce n'est naturellement qu'une hypothèse. Il se peut bien que סדרא אחרינא indique un recueil massorétique distinct qui à un moment donné

---

12. Selon E. Ehrentreu (*Untersuchungen über die Massora*, Hanovre 1925, 73-87), la *ʾoklah* primitive se composait de 150 listes, comme le Psautier se compose de 150 Psaumes. Sa démonstration relève de la pure et simple phantasie.

13. Présence ou absence de la conjonction *waw*, échanges entre les prépositions *bet* et *kaf*, *qeré/ketiv*, et ainsi de suite.

14. On enregistre pour la plupart des formes qui ne diffèrent d'autres formes que par leur vocalisation, en protégeant évidemment la forme plus rare (par exemple, les וַיָּבֵא *hifil* moins nombreux des וַיָּבֹא *qal*.

a été joint au premier. Remarquons toutefois que le plus ancien témoin dont nous disposons, Firkovic Ebr. II B 1554, contient déjà les deux parties.

Remarquons encore que les listes de la seconde partie de la '*oklah we'oklah* sont attestées en grande majorité dans les marges de manuscrits anciens, tels le code du Caire ou celui de St. Pétersbourg B 19A. Ce sont donc des listes anciennes et de bonne qualité, ainsi que le lecteur pourra aisément constater.

Qu'elle appartienne ou non à la collection '*oklah we'oklah*, la seconde partie du manuscrit de Halle renferme donc une source massorétique de grande valeur, qui mérite certainement d'être connue et étudiée.

## Méthode d'édition

Mon édition ne présente pas une transcription du manuscrit de Halle, mais sa reproduction obtenue par le *scanner*.

J'ai procédé de la façon suivante. J'ai d'abord tiré du microfilm du manuscrit[15] des photocopies d'excellente qualité. Je les ai ensuite passées au *scanner*, obtenant une image digitalisée de chaque page. J'ai ensuite découpé à l'ordinateur chaque liste et l'ai importée dans le texte, en lui appliquant un fond gris clair pour rendre la lecture moins fatiguante.

Le manuscrit est écrit clairement, en beaux caractères carrés, et se lit en général très facilement. Par endroits j'ai été obligé d'enlever les traces de l'écriture du revers de la feuille qui se montre à travers le parchemin trop mince. J'ai enlevé aussi naturellement les taches et redressé les lignes inclinées. Je tiens à préciser que je n'ai pas voulu faire une édition facsimilé, mais uniquement éviter les fautes de transcription.

---

15. Mis aimablement à ma disposition par D. Barthélemy.

En découpant les listes j'ai laissé dehors les abréviations des livres bibliques placées dans les marges du manuscrit par une main postérieure. Je les ai remplacées par mes références bibliques modernes (livre, chapitre et verset). Pour indiquer les livres j'ai employé les sigles latins, pour faciliter la consultation de l'ouvrage par des lecteurs ne connaissant pas la langue italienne. A la fin du livre on trouvera un index de tous les versets bibliques cités dans les listes.

J'ai respecté la numérotation du manuscrit, qui est de la main originale du copiste. J'ai cependant ajouté des lettres de l'alphabet[16] pour distinguer les listes à l'intérieur d'une série.

J'ai traduit tous les titres et sous-titres. On en trouvera une liste complète, dans l'ordre du manuscrit, aux pp. 469-483. J'ai renoncé à un index analytique comme celui qu'avait composé Díaz Esteban pour son édition.

### Notes explicatives

Chaque liste est suivie d'une note explicative plus ou moins longue.

Ici j'ai suivi le modèle offert par Ginsburg dans le quatrième volume de son recueil.[17] Ginsburg, dont le travail n'a pas été à mon avis suffisamment apprécié, cherche toujours à expliquer la raison pour laquelle tel phénomène textuel a été enregistré par les massorètes. "The design of this Massorah is ...": on peut évidemment discuter si Ginsburg a toujours bien compris les intentions des massorètes, mais ses suggestions sont en tout cas utiles et pour la plupart valables. Suivant

---

16. J'ai omis les lettres I et O pour éviter toute confusion avec les chiffres 1 et 0. Au § 280, qui réunit quelque chose comme 144 *kelalot*, j'ai dû adopter une sous-numérotation numérique.

17. *The Massorah Translated into English with a Critical and Exegetical Commentary, Being Vol. IV of the Entire Work*, Londres 1905.

son exemple, j'ai cherché chaque fois à interpréter l'intention de la massore, en indiquant le phénomène alternatif (le *hilluf*, en termes massorétiques) contre lequel elle veut mettre en garde les copistes ou les lecteurs. Dans la grande majorité des cas en effet la massore enregistre le phénomène minoritaire, c'est-à-dire les mots moins fréquents et par là plus exposés à être assimilés à d'autres d'usage plus commun.

Après l'indication de l'intention probable de la liste, mes notes signalent les éventuelles fautes ou lacunes,[18] ou essaient d'éclaircir des données ambigues.

Lorsqu'une liste est attestée dans un autre manuscrit de la *'oklah*,[19] j'en informe le lecteur. A la différence de Díaz Esteban, je n'ai pas reporté toutes les variantes textuelles entre les manuscrits, et je me suis limité à indiquer et discuter les divergences les plus marquantes, telles l'absence d'un cas. Le lecteur pourra contrôler mes remarques en consultant pour le manuscrit de Paris[20] l'édition de Frensdorff ou le facsimilé de Löwinger, et pour les manuscrits fragmentaires les vingt-deux reproductions photographiques que j'ai inclues dans mon édition.[21]

---

18. La grande majorité des celles-ci se trouvaient sans doute déjà dans la *Vorlage*. Le copiste du manuscrit de Halle se montre en général très fidèle et scrupuleux.

19. Il y a une soixantaine de listes en commun avec le manuscrit de Paris (onze desquelles se trouvent dans la dernière page de celui-ci, ajoutées par une autre main en petits charactères pour remplir l'espace vide; elles ne font pas partie de la *'oklah* proprement dite), et une autre soixantaine en commun avec le fragment *Firkovic Ebr. II B 1554*, plus une vingtaine de listes éparses avec d'autres fragments de la Genizah.

20. Aux pp. 484-485 on trouvera la table des correspondances entre le manuscrit de Paris et la seconde partie du manuscrit de Halle.

21. On les trouvera aux pages 489-510. Les réproductions du fragment Firkovic ont été réalisées à l'ordinateur à partir des photographies de Kahle conservées à la Biblioteca "P. Kahle" dell'Istituto di Orientalistica dell'Università di Torino, les autres de photographies en possession de Díaz-Esteban. Parmi ces fragments un (Cambridge, Taylor-Schechter D 1,12) a été édité partiellement par

Je n'ai pas utilisé la massore marginale du manuscrit Erfurt III,[22] parce que un bon tiers de ses listes n'est pas clairement lisible en microfilm. Je n'ai pas utilisé non plus ce que G. Weil appelait "la *ʾOkhlah* de Lévita",[23] c'est-à-dire la collection de listes massorétiques copiées au début du manuscrit de Munich[24] du *sefer zikronot* de Elie Lévita. A la différence de Weil, j'estime en effet qu'il ne s'agit pas là d'une copie de la *ʾoklah*, mais d'une composition personnelle de Lévita utilisant sans doute un manuscrit de la *ʾoklah*.[25]

Mes notes terminent toujours avec l'indication des parallèles massorétiques. Je me suis limité aux sources éditées: en ordre chronologique la massore de Yaʿaqov ben Ḥayyim,[26] ensuite le grand recueil de Ginsburg,[27] la massore du manuscrit de Leningrad éditée par G. Weil[28]

---

Kahle (*Masoreten des Westens I*, Stuttgart 1927, 29-30) et (presque) entièrement par G. Weil ("Un fragment de *Okhlah* palestinienne", *Annual of the Leeds University Oriental Society* 3 [1961-1962], 68-80). A mon avis seulement le *verso* de ce rouleau contient des listes tirées de la *ʾoklah weʾoklah*.

22. Actuellement Staatsbibliothek Preussischer Kulturbesitz, or. fol. 1213.

23. "Listes massorétiques tibériennes quantifiées antérieures à la *ʾOkhlah* inscrites sur un fragment de palimpseste opistographe d'origine grecque", *Textus* 12 (1985), 101.

24. Bayerische Staatsbibliothek, Heb. 74/I, ff. 12-74.

25. En tout cas, il n'y a que douze listes en commun entre la compilation de Levita et la seconde partie de la *ʾoklah* de Halle.

26. Editée dans la Bible Rabbinique de Venise, voll. 4, 1524-1525. La comparaison avec la seconde partie de la *ʾoklah* montre à l'évidence que b. Ḥayyim a connu et utilisé celle-ci. On constate en effet que beaucoup des listes paraissent dans la massore finale de b. Ḥayyim exactement dans la même succession que dans la seconde partie de la *ʾoklah* de Halle.

27. *The Massorah Compiled from Manuscripts, Alphabetically and Lexically arranged*, voll. 3, Londres 1880-1885. Un certain nombre de listes vient de la seconde partie de la *ʾoklah* de Halle: dix-huit dans le premier volume (selon la déclaration explicite de Ginsburg dans son commentaire) et un nombre difficile à précise dans le second (pour lequel nous n'avons pas le commentaire de Ginsburg).

28. *Massorah Gedolah iuxta codicem Leningradensem B 19 a*, Rome 1971. J'ai inclues d'autres éditions de Weil: "Quatre fragments de la Massorah Magna

et celle du manuscrit du Caire éditée par l'équipe de Madrid.[29]

J'avais déjà terminé mon travail quand je suis venu en possession de *The Masora Magna to the Pentateuch by Shemuel ben Yaʿaqov (Ms.* למ) éditée et expliquée par M. Breuer.[30] Je regrette de n'avoir pas pu insérer dans mon édition les parallèles entre la seconde partie de la *ʾoklah* et la massore de ce manuscrit.[31]

## Contenu de la seconde partie du *sefer ʾoklah weʾoklah*

Je vais donner maintenant un aperçu du contenu de la seconde partie de la *ʾoklah weʾoklah*.

Les §§ 1-40 sont des ensembles de listes. Chaque ensemble réunit des listes portant sur tel mot ou telle racine, les disposant par ordre décroissant selon le nombre des cas catalogués en chacune.[32] Voyons par exemple les seize listes regroupées dans le § 23: 7 וּבָרוּךְ, 4 בֵּרְכוּ, 4 בְּרָכָתֵי, 3 תְּבֹרַךְ 3 מְבֹרָךְ 3 וּבָרַךְ 3 וּבֵרַךְ, 3 וּלְבָרֶךְ, 4 יְבֹרַךְ, 4 בְּרֹכוֹת, 2 וּבְרָכוּ 2 וּבְרָכָה 2 וּלְבָרְכוֹ, 2 בְּרוּךְ, 2 וַיְבָרֶךְ, et un certain nombre de mots *hapax*, tous de la racine ברך.

Les §§ 1-40 couvrent presque la moitié de la seconde partie de la *ʾoklah*. Suivent des listes qui traitent des formes brèves ou longues des noms propres (§§ 41-64), puis des mots qui terminent par la lettre *nun* (§§ 66-72) ou *mem* (§§ 73-76), ou par le *hé* de direction (§§ 77-88).

---

babylonienne", *Textus* 3 (1963), 74-120; "La Massorah Magna babylonienne des Prophètes", *ibid.* 163-170; "Nouveaux fragments inédits de la Massorah Magna babylonienne", *Textus* 6 (1968), 75-105.

29. *El Códice de Profetas de El Cairo, Edición de su texto y masoras*, tt. 8, Madrid 1979-1992 (Textos y Estudios Cardenal Cisneros 20, 26, 30, 31, 36, 37, 44, 51).

30. Voll. 2, New York 1992 (The Manfred and Anne Lehmann Foundation Series 16).

31. Il est assez surprenant que Breuer n'en donne pas les généralités, se limitant à dire qu'il est en relation à ל (= Leningradensis).

32. On trouve cette disposition déjà dans les dernières listes de la première

Nous trouvons par la suite une série de listes qui traitent de la présence ou absence de la conjonction *waw* en début de verset (§§ 89-105), ainsi que de la lettre *hé* en fin de verset (§§ 106-107). Cette série s'achève avec la liste des mots qui paraissent deux fois dans la Bible, une fois en début et une fois en fin de verset (§ 109).

Après cela nous rencontrons une série de listes qui enregistrent des variations entre mots ou phrases semblables, en toute la Bible ou en contextes plus restreints (§§ 110-138). C'est ici que l'on trouve le plus grand nombre de listes en commun avec la *ʾoklah* de Paris.

La dernière série est une sorte de miscellanées où l'on trouve des listes qui ne sont pas regroupées selon leur contenu, mais selon le nombre de. cas qu'elles énumèrent. On y trouve par exemple six listes à 4 cas (§§ 186-190), douze à 3 cas (§§ 193-202), neuf à 4 cas (§§ 203-210), six à 5 cas (§§ 211-215), trois à 6 cas (§§ 216-218), trois à 10 cas (§§ 230-232), six à 7 cas (§§ 238-243), cinq à 6 cas (§§ 244-248), dix à 5 cas (§§ 249-251 et 253-259), six à 4 cas (§§ 260-265), trente-sept à 3 cas (§§ 286-322) et enfin seize à 2 cas (§§ 328-343). Entre les §§ 279 et 280 on rencontre une longue liste, non numérotée,[33] qui rassemble des *kelalot* ("règles"):[34] il s'agit pour la plupart d'exceptions ("toute la Bible ..., sauf un ..."). Cette liste a été probablement interpolée à partir d'une autre source massorétique.

Si l'on compare la composition de la seconde partie de la *ʾoklah* avec celle de la première partie,[35] on constate la même absence de plan. Il n'y a que des blocs juxtaposés sans aucune logique. On peut reconnaître un plan ou quelque chose de semblable seulement à

---

partie: cf. Díaz Esteban, §§ 152-155, 158, 164-170.

33. Pour des raison purement pratiques, je l'ai unifiée avec la suivante, attribuant à tout l'ensemble le n° 280.

34. Au nombre de 144, selon mon compte.

35. Cf. Díaz Esteban, *Sefer 'Oklah we-'Oklah*, LXV-LXVI.

l'intérieur de chaque bloc.[36] On se demande en outre si les blocs eux-mêmes sont l'oeuvre du compilateur (ou des compilateurs) du recueil ou bien s'il existaient déjà comme tels, peut-être dans la tradition orale.

La '*oklah we'oklah* n'est donc pas un recueil ordonné. Il n'est pas non plus exhaustif. Pourquoi par exemple rassembler 63 *hapax* de יצא (§ 2 U) et aucun de קום? Ou encore pourquoi inclure dans la série קום les 2 לַהֲקִימוֹ (§ 4 G), קֵימוֹ (§ 4 H), וְלֹא קָם (§ 4 J), et non les 2 תְּקִימוּ, וַהֲקִמֹתָ, וּבְקוּמָה et קָמֶיךָ? On pourrait multiplier les exemples. Il est évident que le compilateur n'a pas eu l'intention de réunir toutes les listes massorétiques existantes.

## Le but de la '*oklah we'oklah*

Cela nous amène à nous poser la question suivante: pourquoi a-t-on fait le recueil '*oklah we'oklah*? Quelle a été exactement l'intention qui a animé ses auteurs?

Répondons d'abord à une autre question: quel est l'avantage majeur qu'offrent les listes de la '*oklah* par rapport aux listes copiées dans les marges d'un manuscrit biblique? Il ne consiste pas selon moi dans le regroupement des listes en tant que tel, mais dans la précision des informations contenues en elles, c'est-à-dire dans les *simanin*. Si l'on compare les listes de la '*oklah* aux listes copiées dans les marges du manuscrit du Caire, force est de constater que celles de la '*oklah* fournissent des indications plus claires. Lorsque le *siman* est en effet constitué par un seul mot, il est évidemment moins facile de repérer le verset correspondant. Les listes de la '*oklah* offrent[37] à coté du *siman* traditionnel constitué par un seul mot-clé l'*incipit* du verset cor-

---

36. Voyons par exemple dans le premier bloc les antonymies entre les racines בוא (§ 1) et יצא (§ 2), ישב (§ 3) et קום (§ 4), נתן (§ 5) et לקח (§ 6), צוה (§ 11) et שמע (§ 12), ou bien la synonimie אמר (§ 9) et דבר (§ 10). Mais ce sont des faits isolées.

37. A quelques exceptions près.

respondant, ce qui simplifie notablement le travail du massorète. Il est également évident que des *simanin* doubles (mot-clé plus *incipit*)[38] ne peuvent être normalement copiés dans les marges d'un manuscrit biblique, pour des raisons d'espace. Je crois que la ʾ*oklah* est née essentiellement pour répondre à l'exigence d'une plus grande clarté dans l'indication des cas.

Le *siman* double est donc un trait distinctif de la ʾ*oklah* *weʾoklah*.[39] Cela est important quand on se trouve devant un manuscrit fragmentaire. Comment savoir si c'est une ʾ*oklah* ou un autre recueil massorétique? Selon G. Weil, "les manuscrits de la *Okhlah we-Okhlah* sont reconnaissables à la disposition particulière des listes, qui suivent l'ordre numérique des chiffres attribués à chacune d'elles, sans qu'il apparaisse entre elles de lien ou de plan particulier".[40] A la disposition particulière des listes (j'entends par là une correspondance suffisamment marquée avec les manuscrits déjà connus comme appartenant à la ʾ*oklah*), je propose d'ajouter les *simanin* doubles.[41]

La ʾ*oklah* n'est qu'un recueil. La massore existait déjà et fonctionnait déjà. Lorsque la ʾ*oklah* a vu la lumière,[42] les listes massorétiques

---

38. Ces deux éléments ne sont pas contemporains. L'*incipit* est venu après le mot-clé, dont il est le complément explicatif et interprétatif. Il faut tenir compte de cette distance temporelle quand on se trouve en face de contradictions entre les deux éléments.

39. La ʾ*oklah* de Paris présente une série de listes (Frensdorff §§ 274-365), qui se distinguent des autres en ceci qu'elle offre des *simanin* simples et non doubles. Je crois qu'elles viennent d'une source particulière, étrangère à la tradition de la ʾ*oklah* *weʾoklah*.

40. "Un fragment de *Okhlah* palestinienne", 69. Relevons toutefois que le critère numérique n'est pas le seul. Une bonne partie des listes de la premiére partie de la ʾ*oklah* est alphabétique, sans aucune indication numérique.

41. C'est bien leur absence qui me fait douter de l'appartenance à la ʾ*oklah* de certains fragments cités par Díaz Esteban.

42. Probablement au IXme siècle (cf. I. Yeivin, *Introduction to the Tiberian Masorah*, Chico 1980 [Masoretic Studies 5], 130).

étaient déjà établies et se transmettaient soit oralement soit par écrit dans les marges des manuscrits bibliques. Díaz Esteban affirme que "las listas recogidas en los márgenes de los manuscritos bíblicos no son los ladrillos con los que luego se construyó el edificio de la Masora, sino por el contrario, son fragmentos de las listas componentes del *Sefer 'Oklah*".[43] Je ne partage pas son opinion: à mon avis, la ʾ*oklah* n'a pas engendré les listes massorétiques, mais les a regroupées et rendues plus claires en les munissant de références bibliques plus complètes. J'admets toutefois qu'il y a eu aussi un mouvement de retour, et que des listes de la ʾ*oklah* ont été copiées (en forme plus ou moins abrégée) dans les marges des manuscrits bibliques.

Concernant les *simanin*, une autre remarque s'impose. Díaz Esteban a consacré la dernière partie de son introduction aux rapports entre la ʾ*oklah* et le *textus receptus*.[44] Sa conclusion est la suivante: "los simanin o fragmentos de versículo que se hallan en las obras masoréticas muestran frecuentemente variantes textuales distintas del texto masorético recibido. Tales variantes deben ser tenidas en cuenta por la crítica textual: debido a su propria congruencia interna y a que comparadas con las fuentes de variantes admitidas por la erudición bíblica muestran análogos fenómenos".[45] Là encore je ne partage pas son opinion. Ce sont les règles de la massore qui entrent en ligne de compte pour la critique textuelle de la Bible hébraïque, non pas le texte des *simanin* comme tel, qui est soumis aux mêmes accidents de copie que n'importe quel texte manuscrit.

---

43. *Sefer 'Oklah we-'Oklah*, LXI.

44. *Sefer 'Oklah we-'Oklah*, LXVII-LXXV. Díaz Esteban a compté environ 8000 variantes textuelles dans la première partie de la ʾ*oklah* de Halle.

45. *Sefer 'Oklah we-'Oklah*, LXXV. Voir aussi du même auteur "The *sefer Oklah we-Oklah* As a Source of Not Registered Textual Variants", *ZAW* 70 (1958), 250-253.

## La *'oklah we'oklah* et la vocalisation de la Bible

Dans ses notes au § 5 de son édition (alphabet de mots qui se rencontrent deux fois, une fois *mille'el* et une fois *millera'*), Díaz Esteban affirme: "En un texto escrito con vocales y acentos, esta lista no tendría razón de ser, puesto que con leer la palabra, ya se sabría dónde habría de ponerse el acento, y cómo han de leerse las vocales. Es muy verosímil, por tanto, que esta lista se retrotraiga a un tiempo en el que la vocalización aún no estaba en uso entre los hebreos, y la acentuación-vocalización de estas palabras había de saberse de memoria y aprenderse de viva voz".[46]

La seconde partie de la *'oklah we'oklah* confirme ce jugement de Díaz Esteban. La plupart des ses listes enregistre en effet des mots qui ont la même base consonantique (homoconsonantiques, si l'on accepte le néologisme) mais une prononciation différente par rapport à d'autres mots d'usage plus fréquent. Les וַיָּבֵא sont moins nombreux que les וַיָּבֹא, les לָצֵאת que les לָצֵאת, et ainsi de suite. Ces listes remontent sans doute à une époque où la prononciation des mots était encore conservée par la tradition orale, avant d'être fixée par écrit selon les différents systèmes des orientaux et des occidentaux.

La massore ne travaillait donc pas uniquement au service des copistes du texte sacré, mais également de ses lecteurs. Pour elle la prononciation n'était pas moins importante que l'écriture. Ce fait est trop souvent ignoré ou negligé. Les massorètes ne comptaient pas que les lettres.[47] Ils comptaient aussi les occurrences de telle ou telle prononciation, protégeant toujours logiquement la vocalisation moins fréquente.

---

46. *Sefer 'Oklah we-'Oklah*, 21.

47. Notons à ce propos que les listes de la seconde partie de la *'oklah* montrent très peu d'intérêt pour les écritures pleines et défectives.

Il faut évidemment vérifier jusqu'à quel point la tradition de lecture est unitaire. J'ai l'impression qu'elle ne l'est pas moins que la tradition d'écriture. Certes il y a eu des débats et des discussions, mais dans l'ensemble il faut admettre que la prononciation de la Bible a été transmise aussi fidèlement que son texte consonantique.

L'exégè se est encore aujourd'hui largement prisonnière d'un préjugé négatif vis-à-vis de la vocalisation massorétique. Voyons par exemple le commentaire aux Psaumes de M. Dahood pour la Anchor Bible,[48] où il se vante d'avoir corrigé seulement huit fois le texte consonantique du Psautier, alors qu'à chaque pas il propose de nouvelles vocalisations basées sur les parallèles avec la littérature ougaritique. Cette différence de traitement entre le texte consonantique et la prononciation n'est pas historiquement fondée, puisque la massore a aussi soigneusement conservé l'un que l'autre. On les accepte ensemble ou on les refuse ensemble.

Certains savants pensent que l'édition critique de la Bible hébraïque ne devrait comprendre que le texte consonantique, les voyelles étant un élément d'ordre interprétatif, ne faisant pas partie du "texte" proprement dit.[49] Là encore cette division entre consonnes et voyelles ne me semble pas justifiée. Pourquoi les voyelles ne feraient-elles pas partie du texte biblique? Le fait qu'elles ont été notées par écrit plus tard ne signifie pas pour autant qu'elles soient un élément adventice ou tardif. La Bible a toujours été lue, même avant Aaron ben Asher. La tradition de lecture est aussi ancienne que la tradition d'écriture. Les massorètes n'ont pas inventé la vocalisation, mais seulement des systèmes de ponctuation. Il est certainement légitime de vouloir reconstituer critiquement le texte consonantique dans une forme

---

48. Voll. 3, Garden City 1965-1970 (The Anchor Bible 16-17-17a).

49. En Italie nous avons eu récemment deux éditions critiques qui ne présentent que les consonnes: P. G. Borbone, *Il libro del profeta Osea*, Turin 1990 (Quaderni di Henoch 2); G. Garbini, *Cantico dei Cantici*, Brescia 1992 (Biblica. Testi e studi 2).

plus ancienne que celle qui a servi de base au travail des massorètes. J'admets que la Bible hébraïque et la Bible massorétique ne sont pas exactement la même chose.[50] Cela ne signifie pas pourtant que les voyelles et les accents soient à considérer comme des éléments purement interprétatifs, étrangers au texte en tant que tel.

Dans l'histoire du texte de la Bible hébraïque il y a deux grand piliers: la fixation écrite du texte consonantique et la fixation écrite de la prononciation. Le pont qui les unit est la massore. Son élement le plus précieux est la tradition de lecture qu'elle a gardé au long des siècles. Je termine mon exposé par une invitation à l'étudier critiquement et à l'apprécier correctement.

---

50. Je dirais que la Bible massorétique est la forme mûre et achevée de la Bible hébraïque. Avant Aaron ben Asher, la Bible n'avait pas encore été mise entièrement par écrit.

# ERASED *GA'YOT* IN CODEX LENINGRADENSIS

Harold P. Scanlin
United Bible Societies

The publishers of *Biblia Hebraica Stuttgartensia (BHS)* are undertaking a completely new edition to be known as *Biblia Hebraica Quinta (BHQ)*. This project is a natural outgrowth of the Hebrew Old Testament Text Project sponsored by the United Bible Societies for the purpose of providing for its translation teams throughout the world a thorough analysis of textual issues in the Hebrew Bible which may be encountered in the translation process. An international team of Biblical scholars, headed by Dominique Barthélemy met annually for over 10 years and published their interim findings in *Preliminary and Interim Report of the Hebrew Old Testament Text Project* in five volumes. Barthélemy has now also published three of the five final report volumes in the series *Critique textuelle d'Ancient Testament.*[1]

In the process of their work, the HOTTP Committee recognized that the abundance of newly discovered manuscript evidence, especially the Dead Sea Scrolls, and a new appreciation for the text history of the Hebrew Bible and the ancient versions called for a thoroughgoing revision of *BHS*. A new international and interfaith team of textual scholars were brought together to begin work on this new edition. A sample fascicle will be published in 1997 and it is hoped that the entire Hebrew Bible will be published in the early part of the first decade of the 21st century.

---

[1] *1. Josué, Juges, Ruth, Samuel, Rois, Chroniques, Esdras, Néhémie, Esther.* (Orbis Biblicus et Orientalis, 50/1). Fribourg, Switzerland & Göttingen, 1982. *2. Isaïe, Jérémie, Lamentations* (Orbis Biblicus et Orientalis, 50/2). Fribourg, Switzerland & Göttingen, 1986. *Tome 3. Ézéchiel, et les 12 Prophètes* (Orbis Biblicus et Orientalis, 50/3). Fribourg, Switzerland & Göttingen, 1992.

The Hebrew text of *BHQ* will present a diplomatic edition of L, although it will not be a full diplomatic edition in that it will not represent all orthographic features, e.g. *raphe* and line fillers, and will not attempt to duplicate the line length of the manuscript, although poetic strophing will be based on the hierarchy of the disjunctive accents at least to the first and second level.

The masora will be presented as in L, rather than the expanded treatment by G. E. Weil in *BHS*. However, relevant information found in the Masorah Magna will be given in English in a supplementary commentary volume, which should make masora more accessible to users, especially translators and students. The *simanim* will be transcribed into modern chapter and verse references, a practice already instituted in the new *Miqraot Gedolot* based on the Aleppo Codex and being published by Bar-Ilan U. Press.[2]

The editors of *BHQ* originally considered the possibility of collating the masora of two other ben Asher manuscripts against L. Although this would have been a worthy project, it was soon realized that the publication of such a full collation would be entirely too large for a manual edition such as *BHQ*. However, the editors will still examine at least two other major ben Asher manuscripts and report in the apparatus significant variants in relation to the masora of L.

Abraham Firkovitch (or Firkowitsch, etc.) was the greatest collector of Hebrew manuscripts, both biblical and non-biblical, in the nineteenth century. He was a Karaite Jew, at least in his earlier years of his career and was an outspoken critic of rabbinic Judaism. Firkovitch had the reputation of falsifying the dates of some records, especially on tombstones, presumably in an effort to bolster the antiquity of the origin of the Karaite sect. There is some evidence that dates were altered, especially on tombstone tracings — for example, a Karaite who reportedly died in the 2nd century CE! — , but the polemic on both sides resulted in numerous overstatements. There is no evidence reported by reputable scholars of Firkovitch's day, nor any that I have seen, that he forged any Biblical texts, although dates on

---

2 מקראות גדלות הכתר, Menachem Cohen, editor. Ramat-Gan:Bar Ilan U., 1992 - .

some colophons may have been altered.  Regrettably, Firkovitch did not provide much information on the provenance of many of the manuscripts he found.[3]  In 1839 Firkovitch brought the magnificent, complete Hebrew Bible codex which we now know as Codex Leningradensis to Odessa.  He had purchased it in Cairo, although he offered no further details on the manuscript's provenance.  Tapani Harviainen, of Finland, has gone through much of the personal correspondence and personal catalog of Firkovitch, which is in St. Petersburg along with his manuscript collections.  In a personal conversation, Harviainen reported that he has as yet found no references to B19[a].  (See also Harviainen, 1991.)  B19[a] was first described in some detail by Moses Pinner in a *Nachtrag* (pp. 81-92) to his *Prospectus der Odessaer Gesellschaft für Geschichte und Alterthümer gehörenden ältesten hebräischen und rabbinischen Manuscripte* (Odessa, 1845).

Firkovitch sold his first collection of manuscripts to the Public Library at St. Petersburg, and the second collection was acquired by the same library in 1876, two years after Firkovitch's death.  The codex was assigned the designation B19[a] by A. Harkavy and H. L. Strack in their *Catalog der hebräischen Bibelhandschriften der Kaiserlichen Öffentlichen Bibliothek in St. Petersburg* (St. Petersburg/Leipzig: Ricker/Hinrichs, 1875), and described in some detail on pages 263 - 274.

Little use seems to have been made of B19[a] by biblical scholars of the late 19th and early 20th century, even though Harkavy and Strack described it as "next to Codex B 3 [the famous Babylonian Codex of the Latter Prophets], the most important of the St. Petersburg Bible manuscripts.  C. D. Ginsburg did not use it in his famous critical edition, although he discusses it in his *Introduction*, pp. 243-244. R. Kittel took no notice of it in the first and second editions of *Biblia Hebraica* (1906, 19).

---

3 Benjamin Richler, *Guide to Hebrew Manuscripts* (Jerusalem: Israel Academy of Sciences and Humanities) provides a concise description of Firkovitch's work and his collections now in St. Petersburg, pp. 51-52, 98-101. See also Bezalel Narkiss's new intorduction to the reprint edition of *Illuminations from Hebrew Bibles of Leningrad*, originally published by David Günzburg and Vladimir Stassoff (Jerusalem: Bialik Institute and Ben-Zvi, 1990), pp. 18-31

While Paul Kahle was in Leningrad in 1926 at the public library studying their famous collection of Hebrew manuscripts, Rudolf Kittel wrote to inform Kahle that he was preparing to work on a third edition of *Biblia Hebraica* and felt that it would be necessary to again print the traditional ben Chaiyim text of the Rabbinic Bibles. Kahle, however, persuaded him to base the new edition on B19$^a$ as a superior text of the ben Asher tradition.

After Kittel agreed with Kahle's proposal arrangements were made to send the codex to Leipzig for the editors' work on the new edition. Kahle explains, ". . . das 1926 für zwei Jahre auf meine Bitte hin nach Deutschland gesandt worden war. Leider sind [Gottfried] Quell's Aufzeichnungen, die er für Rudolf Kittel angefertigt hatte, noch nicht wieder aufgefunden worden. . . . Hoffentlich wird es möglich sein, die Aufzeichnungen von Professor Quell wieder zu finden und die Korrekturen in der photographischen Aufnahmen des Lenigradensis zu erkennen."[4] Regrettably, Quell's notes do not seem to have survived. In the Vorwort to the first published fascicle of *BHK* (Isaiah, 1929), the editors hoped to utilize all three famous ben Asher codexes, L, A, and C. They obtained a set of photographs of C just before the publication of *BHK* began, but any hope of obtaining photographs of A were abandoned by the time of the publication of the complete *BHK* in 1937.

> Rudolf Kittel and I had hoped to be able to replace the Leningrad MS. L., which was used as the basis of the *Biblia Hebraica* in the course of our work, with the model codex of ben Asher himself which is kept in the synagogue of the Sephardim in Aleppo. That has not been possible since the owners of the codex would not hear of a photographic copy. Moreover, the personal representations made by Gotthold Weil and Hellmut Ritter in Aleppo have had no success.[5]

---

4 *Der hebräische Bibeltext seit Franz Delitzsch* (Stuttgart: W. Kohlhammer, 1961), pp. 77-78.

5 *Biblia Hebraica*, Rudolph Kittel and Paul Kahle, editors, p. xxix.

A set of photographs was made in Leipzig before the manuscript was returned to Leningrad. According to Kahle the Leipzig photographs were destroyed in World War II, although reduced size duplicate photographs were made and taken to Bonn by Kahle. The whereabouts of this set of photographs cannot be documented.[6]

For the preparation of a revised edition of the Bible Society's Hebrew Bible, to be known as *Biblia Hebraica Stuttgartensia*, the manuscript was refilmed through the agency of the state library in Berlin, according to a report given to me by Hans Peter Rüger, coordinating editor of *BHS*. This is confirmed by a statement made by Kahle in a letter dated May 23, 1956, presumably sent to Díez Macho, since the letter is quoted by him, but otherwise without attribution (1965:31). Kahle's statement is quite surprising, since he seems to have come to devalue B19ª: "I had a card from Professor Eissfeldt [who was officially Kittel's successor as editor of Biblia Hebraica, and was responsible for some of the initial work on *BHS*] that the Leningrad Library has sent a microfilm from the ben Asher Bible Ms. B19ª. the Academy of Berlin has asked for the Ms. itself in order to make a photography with all specialities. I think that the problems are now different and the Leningrad Codex is not of such an importance as the people in Germany believe." What can be made of Kahle's statement? It is clear from Díez Macho's account of Kahle's research interests in the 1950's that Kahle had returned to his earlier interest in the Babylonian Hebrew Bible tradition and its vocalization system. See, for example, his important *Masoreten des Ostens*. Kahle's lack of involvement in the new *BHS* edition may also have been a factor. In any case, Kahle had also argued that the newly discovered Qumran biblical manuscripts lent support to his theory regarding multiple text types.

The new microfilm made for the work of the *BHS* committee seems to have disappeared in transit from Stuttgart back to Berlin, but a set of photographic copies were made in Tübingen for Rüger's use as continuing editor for the correction and improvement of succeeding editions and printings of *BHS*. In what seems to be a recurring pattern, this set of photographs can no longer be located either, but copies of

---

[6] For further details, see *The Cairo Geniza*, 2nd edition,

the entire manuscript were produced for my use in evaluating the possible reason for discrepancies that were observed when comparing the printed edition of *BHS*, The Makor facsimile edition, and Dotan's readings for his published edition.

Before going on the describe the Makor and Dotan works, we note that another microfilm of B19$^a$ was prepared in 1958 (or 1956) in conjunction with a major project undertaken by Abraham I. Katsh, then at New York University, to film Hebrew manuscript treasures of the Soviet Union. Katsh made two trips to the Soviet Union in 1956 and 1958 and reported that he and his colleague microfilmed over 500 manuscripts, some of which were only fragments. Eighty eight reduced facsimiles of B19$^a$, (folios 447v to 491v) are reproduced in part 2 of Katsh's catalog, *Ginze Russiyah* (New York: New York Univ. Library of Judaica and Hebraica, 1957-58). The quality of these reproductions are only fair, but they do not show some of the damage to be seen in other reproductions. Unfortunately, this microfilm is currently not accessible and is no longer housed at New York University.

In 1970, Makor Publishing of Jerusalem, issued a facsimile edition of B19$^a$, in three volumes, with an introduction by D. S. Loewinger. The edition was said to be limited to 135 copies, but there seems to have been at least two different printings, with some minor differences. One printing is undated, but presumably issued in 1970; the second printing is dated 1971. In the former, page 2 is blank, in the latter, page 2 is the manuscript page containing ancient ownership information. Several pages of reproductions in the earlier edition are cropped with loss of text, in the later these pages show more text. Loewinger's introduction offers no clue regarding the preparation of this facsimile edition, but it is quite apparent that the work was done from a set of existing photographs that show visible signs of wear, including scratches and loss of film emulsion. For example, there is a clear crack on plate I.155, and the loss of emulsion on I.188. There is some indication that the photographs used were glass plates. The plates of B19$^a$ reproduced by Yeivin appear to exhibit similar characteristics.[7]  Yeivin plate 19 (= Makor III.309) appears to have

---

[7] Israel Yeivin, מבחר כתבי־יד של המקרא (Jerusalem: Akademon 1972).

cracked completely through on the horizontal, and a piece of film (glass?) is missing from the lower right margin. I have not been able to trace the whereabouts of the photos which Kahle had made from the Leipzig filming; the Makor edition may have had access to this set of photos.

Aron Dotan considered the presentation of B19[a] by the editors of *BHK* inadequate because of "faulty readings in the manuscripts." In Dotan's opinion, the first several fascicles of the new *BHS* edition contained "mistaken readings of the manuscript . . . even more numerous than in its predecessor. (1976:1105-1106)" Dotan published a new edition of the Hebrew Bible based on B19[a], תורה נביאים וכתובים *The Holy Scriptures accurately edited according to the vocalization, accents and masora of Aaron ben Moses be Asher in the Leningrad Codex* (Tel-Aviv and Ramat-Gan: "Adi" Publishers and Bar-Ilan U., 1976). The subtitle supports Dotan's view that B19[a] is a reliable witness to the ben Asher text. In comparing the other great ben Asher manuscript, the Aleppo codex, Dotan concludes, "In spite of the differences between them, which are inconsequential, the two manuscripts clearly belong to one school which in matters of vocalization, accents and Masora differ substantially from other texts (1976: 1105)." Although Dotan made some concessions to a true diplomatic edition of B19[a] in the interest of usage in the religious community, he carefully documents these changes and offers an extended discussion of the issues involved in reading the manuscript. Recent studies of the photographs of B19[a] indicate that Dotan's edition contains numerous improved readings in comparison to the printed edition of *BHS*.

It was clear that new high quality photographs of B19[a] would be an invaluable contribution to the general study of the Hebrew Bible as well as an essential tool for the editors of the new edition of Biblia Hebraica. Only in this way could the anomalies uncovered in the comparison of existing reproductions be resolved. In response to a number of requests from the academic community and through my urging on behalf of the Bible Societies, the Ancient Biblical Manuscript Center (ABMC), Claremont, CA, in cooperation with West Semitic Research, Rolling Hills Estates, CA, undertook this major project. Through careful and lengthy negotiations, arrangements were made with the custodians of B19ᵃ, then known as the Saltykov-Shchedrin State Public Library of Leningrad (now the National Public Library of St. Petersburg) to film the entire manuscript in high resolution color photographs. These photographs and microfilm copies are now available to the academic community and form the basis for the preparation of *Biblia Hebraica Quinta*. A two color facsimile edition is expected to be published March 1996 by Eerdmans, Grand Rapids, MI. It is also hoped that a high quality full color facsimile edition can also be published, primarily intended for the large research library. In the meantime, ABMC has produced a full set of color transparencies for the *BHQ* committee and is prepared to provide high quality prints of selected pages for interested scholars.

One of the most surprising results of the comparison of *BHS* with the Makor plates and photocopies made from the microfilm used by the editors of *BHS* committee was a large number of discrepancies between the two sets of photographic images. In most cases the discrepancies could be accounted for by the relatively poor quality of both sets of reproductions. However, other discrepancies were completely anomalous.

A particularly striking example is found in Hosea 9:15. There is absolutely no trace of a *qames* under the שׂ of שׂרֵיהֶם in the film copy used by the *BHS* editors; accordingly, *BHS* did not vocalize the שׂ and added a *sic.* note. The Makor edition, however, shows that there is a *qames* under the שׂ. The new photographs show a *qames* even more clearly. Naturally, *BHQ* will drop the *sic.* note and vocalize שָׂ.

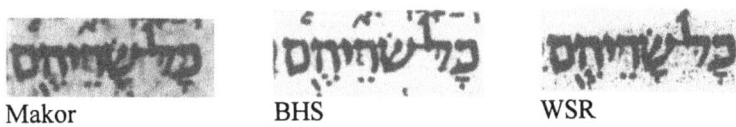

Makor             BHS             WSR

There are hundreds of other examples of apparent discrepancies in the photographic images, most of which are not nearly as striking as this example. In fact, virtually all involve the teamim.

A list of over 600 discrepancies was submitted to Dr. Rüger, who reviewed them and changed the text of *BHS* in the fourth edition (1990) in about 250 cases. The rest were considered too ambiguous to make a definitive evaluation. It was decided that the remaining 200 +

discrepancies could only be resolved on the basis of a careful examination of the high quality color transparencies. The author examined the transparencies at West Semitic Research in Rolling Hills Estates, CA, and was joined by Marilyn Lundberg of the Ancient Biblical Manuscript Center, who had assisted in the photography in Leningrad, and by Robert Bascom. As a result of this initial examination, additional changes have been recommended in the subsequent printings of *BHS* and/or the text of *BHQ*.[8] Prof. Adrian Schenker, coordinating editor of *BHQ*, will examine the B19ᵃ transparencies to verify and correct the readings presented in *BHS*. It is hoped that these improved readings can be made in future printings of *BHS*, so that the results of this research can be made available to the academic community even before the publication of *BHQ*. A sample fascicle should be published in 1997 and the entire *BHQ* in the first decade of the 21st century. Alan Groves, who was responsible for the original work of cross-checking photographs and electronic files, resulting in the generation of the original list of 600 questioned readings, will also be responsible for correcting the electronic edition of B19ᵃ.

## Erasures in B19ᵃ

It is well known that B19ᵃ exhibits a number of erasures and corrections. Pérez Castro says, "... el Ms. B19ᵃ de Leningrado, por virtud de multitud de correcciones, raspaduras y añadiduras, es decir, su segunda mano, refleja de una manera casi absoluta la puntuación de

---

[8] The author's evaluation may be summarized as follows:

- 250 changes have already been made by H. P. Rüger in *Biblia Hebraica Stuttgartensia*, 4th edition (1990).
- 61 additional changes in *BHS* are clearly necessary.
- 40 problems can be resolved in favor of *BHS*.
- 41 problems remain unresolved, of which
    28 relate to *ga'yot*
    13 need further analysis.
- 16 items relate to typesetting matters (postpositive vs. prepositive *teamim*) in which the typesetting of *BHS* results in some ambiguity.

Aharón Ben Ašer."[9] Dotan, in the introduction to his diplomatic edition of Leningradensis, says, "We ignored erased symbols, since this manuscript was adapted to the ben Asher system, and this accounts for a large part of the erasures. The erased symbols are doubtless important for a study of the history of the text of the Leningrad manuscripts, but for our purposes we are obliged to adopt the final text.."[10]

In comparing the earlier photographs I noticed that there was a category of discrepancies relating to *ga'yot*. There were a number of cases where there appeared to be a *ga'ya* in Makor but not in the *BHS* microfilm, as well as some counter-examples.. It seemed possible that what was seen on the poor quality photos were actually traces of erasures. An examination of the new color photos suggested to me that one of the systematic corrections in B19[a] was the erasure of *ga'yot*. On the other hand, Kittel and Kahle took little notice of any scribal alterations in B19[a]. In fact, they intervened in the "regularization" of the *ga'yot*. "After many lengthy discussions with Paul Kahle I have put the *Metheg* or omitted it in all cases where the editor of L seemed to have good reasons for insertion or omission, and have changed it only where I believed a mistake should be assumed (1937, Pref xxvii). Kahle persuaded Kittel by the time of the appearance of the Psalms fascicle (1930) to place all manuscript *ga'yot* to the left of the vowel, but the added *ga'yot* to the right. This distinction was abandoned in *BHS*: "The addition of . . . Metheg, which is often omitted [in the manuscript] has been discontinued, particularly as in L itself Metheg is found both to the left and to the right of the vowel pointing [indiscriminately, HPS] (Proleg. xii)."

In order to determine if the process of correction of B19[a] included a systematic revision of the use and placement of *ga'yot* it was decided to examine the book of Isaiah as a test book, in part, because Isaiah is extant in both A and C as well. There seem to be at

9 F. Perez Castro, "Una copia del *Codex Hilleli* Colacionada con la Primera Mano del MS.B19A de Leningrado." *Sefarad* 38:1978):18."

10 Aron Dotan, תורה נביאים וכתובים *The Holy Scriptures* (Tel-Aviv/Ramat-Gan: "Adi" and Bar-Ilan U., 1976),

least six cases of possible *ga'ya* erasures in Isaiah. In each case the Aleppo codex has no *ga'ya*.[11]

**7:20**

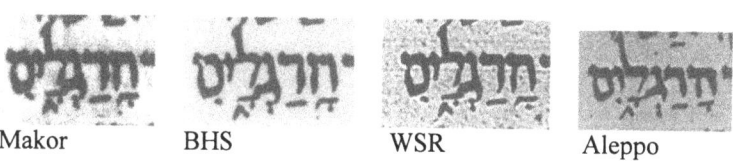

| Makor | BHS | WSR | Aleppo |

There appear to be traces of an accent to the left of the *qames* under the ה in both the Makor edition and the microfilm used by the BHS committee. However, the West Semitic Research (WSR) filming shows here, and even more noticeably in the color original, that there are only very slight traces of two tiny spots of ink and the parchment texture between the spots suggests an erasure. The Aleppo codex clearly lacks any accent, although Breuer places a *ga'ya* here in his printed edition based on Aleppo. There is no *ga'ya* in the Aleppo-based *Miqraot Gedolot* being published by Bar-Ilan University.

**14:27**

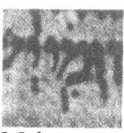 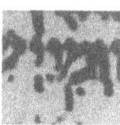  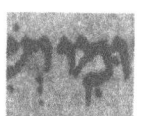

| Makor | BHS | WSR | Aleppo |

The BHS microfilm shows a probable *ga'ya* beneath the ו, but its placement slightly to the right of the descending stroke is somewhat unusual. Nevertheless, Makor also shows a sign, although in physical appearance it looks more like an anomalous *shewa*. The WSR color

---

11 In Breuer's printed edition of the Hebrew Bible which is based on the Aleppo codex, occasionally there are printed *ga'yot* which do not appear in the manuscript. Breuer's printed edition is generally quite reliable, but it is not clear to me how Breuer applied his analysis of the Aleppo tradition to the use of *teamim* and especially *ga'yot* in the Torah.

image shows that the apparent *ga'ya* is a shade of dark brown which differs from the darker color, usually black, of the ink. The WSR image has been computer enhanced to show both the dark color and the lack of definition to the mark, distinguishing it from the sharpness of the letters and accents in B19ª. Aleppo shows no accent.

---

### 37:10

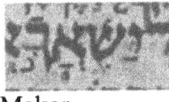 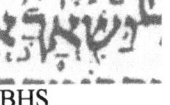 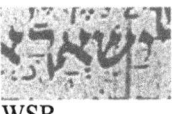 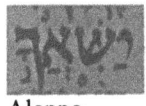

Makor        BHS        WSR        Aleppo

This is a striking example of an apparent *ga'ya* beneath the שׁ. In Makor only a trace of an apparent accent can be seen. In WSR the erasure shows up as a light brown area of a slightly different color and texture in the parchment. This is a well executed erasure, leaving only slight traces of a *ga'ya*. The very small *maqqef* is typical of the B19ª scribe. Aleppo lacks *ga'ya*, and the Bar-Ilan *Miqraot Gedolot*, although Breuer includes it. The *maqqef* occurs at the end of the preceding line.

---

### 40:27

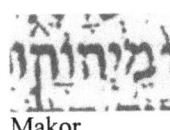  

Makor        BHS        WSR        Aleppo

Traces of a *ga'ya* appear to be under the מ in both Makor and BHS. This page in B19ª is not well preserved, although the deterioration is not a extensive as may be suggested by WSR.

---

**50:2**

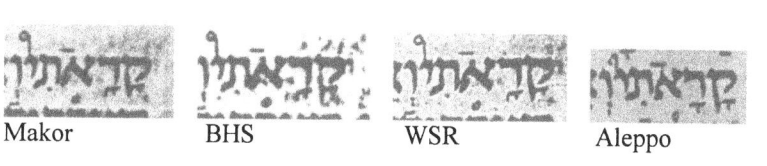

Makor   BHS   WSR   Aleppo

The mark at the lower right of the ר was interpreted by the BHS editors as a *ga'ya*, although their microfilm was especially indistinct here. Makor also appears to read *ga'ya*. The black and white reproduction of WSR does not show that the downstroke at the ר is actually a different color than the adjacent ink and is slightly elongated, atypical of the scribe's *ga'yot*.

---

**61:7**

Makor   BHS   WSR   Aleppo

The erased *ga'ya* under ת has left faint discoloration in WSR. The photography process used in Makor and BHS has transformed this modest discoloration into a surviving *ga'ya*. Note, however, that the mark is less well defined than the usual accent or letter. This is especially true of Makor.

## Other Corrections in Codex L

The tendency of the B19[a] scribe to make corrections toward a ben Asher text may also be seen by comparing his erasures to the list of differences between ben Asher and ben Naphtali listed in Mishael ben Uzziel's *Kitab al-Khilaf* (or *Sefer Hillufim*, The Book of Differences). Although we say "the scribe, i.e. Shmuel ben Yaakov, made the changes, there is no physical evidence in the manuscript itself and its inks to confirm that he, and not a later scribe, actually made the corrections. On the other hand, we do have Shmuel's declaration in his colophon that "It [the manuscript] has been corrected and properly annotated."[12]

Several probable *ga'yot* erasures in Genesis, in fact, correspond to Mishael's *Hillufim*. In 3:3 ben Naphtali places a *ga'ya* under the ה in בתוך.while ben Asher lacks *ga'ya*. B19[a] shows a faint trace of a probable erasure of a *ga'ya*, as seen in all photo reproductions. In 18:26, where ben Naphtali has *ga'ya* under כ in לכל and ben Asher lacks *ga'ya*, it is impossible to detect an erasure, even in the high quality color WSR transparencies, although Perez Castro (1955: 7) notes an erasure. There is trace evidence of an erased *ga'ya* in 25:22 under the initial ו in ויתרצצו, which would again suggest that a ben Naphtali reading has been changed to a ben Asher reading. A clear example of an erased *ga'ya* in conformity with the ben Naphtali to ben Asher adjustment may be seen in Gen 30:16, where the *ga'ya* under the מ in מן has been erased.

*[margin notes: Gen 3:3, Gen 18:26, Gen 25:22, Gen 30:16]*

## The Other extant manuscripts of Shmuel

In another manuscript copied by the scribe of B19[a], Shmuel ben Yaakov, a similar pattern of erasure, especially of *ga'yot* may be seen. In a manuscript designated לם by Mordechai Breuer in his recent publication of the masora magna of this manuscript, "there is evidence of another scribe's hand, which is recognized, among other things, by

---

12 See page 121 for the full text of the colophon.

the many erasures of *ga'yahs* and other signs."[13] According to Breuer there are significantly more light *ga'yot* in Deut. 28:18 - 31:30 in לם than in Aleppo – 190 vs. 50, although the reverse is true in 1 Samuel: לם 50 -- Aleppo 70.[14]

Breuer's designates the manuscript Ms.לם. The ל means that it was written by the same scribe, Shemuel ben Ya'aqov, who wrote B19ª. The ם signifies that this ms may be either earlier (המוקד) or later (המאוחר) than B19ª, a matter that is uncertain, since Ms לם lacks any date. Breuer believes that לם is earlier, since the masora reflects aspects of the Babylonian tradition that is sometimes at variance with the Tiberian tradition, and it would be difficult to imagine that the scribe in the ben Asher tradition would have moved from Tiberian to Babylonian masora characteristics. Breuer hesitates, however, to be conclusive, since there is a significant counter-example in the superior way לם arranges Deut 32 in 69 lines, rather than the 37 line, two column, arrangement of B19ª, which generally does not space the columns at syntactically appropriate places, either.

Breuer does not offer any further information on the provenance of לם. However, Malachi Beit-Arié lists three manuscripts prepared by Shemuel ben Ya'aqov in his enumeration of 9th - 11th century biblical codices (see his recent volume of collected essays, with additions and corrections, *The Makings of the Medieval Hebrew Book* (Jerusalem: Magnes, 1993), pp. 111-112 + 125):

m. 1009     Cairo - MS. Leningrad Public Library, B19ª

n. ca. 1009   [Cairo?] - MS. Cairo, Karaite Synagogue, Bible
                   430 x 387 mm.; 3 columns, 19 lines.

o. ca. 1009   [Cairo?] - MS. Cairo, Karaite Synagogue, Pentateuch.
                   420 x 380 mm.; 3 columns, 17 lines.

To my knowledge, there are no other extant manuscripts known to be prepared by Shemuel ben Ya'aqov. It would appear that Breuer's

---

[13] M. Breuer, *The Masorah Magna to the Pentateuch by Samuel ben Ya'aqov (Ms .לם).* (New York: Manfred and Anne Lehmann Foundation, 1993), p. xix.

[14] *Op. cit.,* xviii.

לם corresponds to either "n" or "o" in Beit-Arié's list. In 1905 Richard Gottheil published a preliminary catalog[15] of "Some Hebrew Manuscripts in Cairo," (*Jewish Quarterly Review* 17:609-655). He identified two manuscripts written by Shemuel ben Yaʿaqov:

14  Pentateuch; 42 x 38 cm., 3 columns, no line count given

27  Former Prophets; 43 x 38 3/4 cm., 3 columns, no line count given.

Gottheil's description of the damaged end of the Former Prophets codex fits well with Breuer's description, which describes even more extensive deterioration. It seems fairly certain that Breuer's part two of לם corresponds to Gottheil 27 and Beit-Arié "n." But is Breuer's Torah volume Beit-Arié "o" (= Gottheil 14) or the Torah part of Beit-Arié n (apparently not seen by Gottheil[16])?

## Conclusion

The special nature of the *ga'ya* as an optional feature, especially in the earlier biblical codexes provides a means for profiling the activity of the punctuator. We have seen that erasures of certain *ga'yot* in B19[a] indicate that a scribe, quite possible Shmuel himself, corrected the manuscript towards a ben Asher standard. As seen in other Shmuel manuscripts, the hegemony of ben Asher was not yet pervasive at the

---

[15] Gottheil laments that circumstances did not permit a more thorough examination and description of the manuscripts. "Persuasion, bakshish and limitless time are needed to overcome the peculiar circumstances attending upon such a labor in Egypt. I found this to be especially true among the Jews. I continually encountered a deadweight, against which everything seemed powerless except one of these forces. In most cases I had to work with a motley horde of sluttish, unkempt, and unwashed men, women, and children peering over my shoulders and into my face. My haste to get away may have been indelicate -- but very necessary in view of my natural wish to carry away no more than I had brought (1905:609)."

[16] Gottheil specifically says of ms. 27; ". . . the four books [Josh., Jdg., Sam., Ki.] were not part of a whole Bible, but were intended to be a volume by themselves (1905: 637)." He does not explain on what basis he makes this statement, although he transcribes the colophon, now virtually illegible according to Breuer, which begins "these four former prophets." This statement would not seem to justify Gottheil's conclusion that this was an independent codex.

beginning of the 11th century, although the rising ascendancy towards that scribal tradition undoubtedly motivated the changes that can now be detected through erasures.

Now that high quality color photographs of L are readily available to researchers, a desideratum is a complete study of the erasures and other scribal alterations in L. Such a study should shed additional light on what transpired during the period that saw the triumph of the ben Asher school. Verification of readings will also enhance the quality of the text that will appear in *BHQ*.

The value of electronic enhancement of manuscripts as a valuable aid to the analysis of erasures has been demonstrated by this study, although examination of manuscripts by the human eye will still be the final arbiter for some crucial readings. It is hoped that first hand access to the Hebrew manuscripts of the Russian National Library in St. Petersburg will continue.

## Postscript

For the sake of convenient reference the text of the colophon, found on leaf 479a, reads:

> Shmuel be Ya'akov wrote and pointed and provided with masora this codex of the Holy Scriptures from the carefully corrected (Würthwein: "corrected and annotated"; Yeivin: "the most exact") texts [הספרים המוגהים המבואר] of Aaron be Moshe ben Asher the teacher, may he rest in the Garden of Eden! It has been corrected and properly annotated.

The order of the books of the Ketuvim in B19ª differs from most modern printed editions of the Hebrew Bible. The order is: Chronicles, Psalms, Job, Proverbs, Megillot (Ruth, Song of Songs, Qoheleth, Lamentations, Esther), Daniel, Ezra-Nehemiah. This is the same order as in the Aleppo codex where extant, although Song 3:12 to the end are lacking.. Even those printed editions based on B19ª, including BHS and Dotan place Chronicles last. Breuer's printed edition based on Aleppo does place Chronicles at the beginning of the Ketuvim.[17] The traditional placement of Chronicles last corresponds to most later biblical manuscripts and the list given in BT Baba Batra 14b.

Some, including Roger Beckwith[18] suggest confirmation of the antiquity of the Chronicles last tradition in a NT passage Matt. 23:35 (and Lk 11:51) which cites "the blood of the righteous from Abel to Zechariah," referring to ancient martyrs from beginning (Genesis) to end (2 Chron 24:20-22, the last martyr mentioned in the Hebrew canon) The argument presents an intriguing possibility but hardly convincing proof.

---

[17] For a list of the manuscripts which place Chronicles at the beginning of the Ketuvim, see the chart on pp. 458-459 in Roger Beckwith, *The Old Testament canon of the New Testament Church* (Eerdmans, 1985).

[18] Beckwith's book (see note 15) has been almost uniformly reviewed as a masterful collection of the relevant data, although his early date for the fixing of the canon of the Hebrew Bible has generally not been accepted.

# Bibliography

Avrin, Leila Rachel Kopstein. 1975. "The Illuminations in the Moshe ben-Asher Codex of 895 C. E." PhD, U. of Michigan.

Beit-Arié, Malachi. 1993. *The Makings of the Medieval Hebrew Book: Studies in palaeography and codicology.* Jerusalem: Magnes.

Beit-Arié, Malachi. 1995. "The Accessibility of the Russian Manuscript Collections: New Perspectives for Jewish Studies." *The Folio* vol. 13, no. 1:1-7.

Breuer Mordechai. 1976. *The Aleppo codex and the accepted text of the Bible.* Jerusalem: Kook. [in Hebrew]

Breuer, Mordechai. 1992. *The Masorah Magna to the Pentateuch by Shemuel ben Ya'aqov (Ms. פל).* New York: Manfred and Anne Lehmann Foundation.

Cassuto, Philippe. 1989. *Qeré-ketib et listes massorétiques dans le manuscrit B19a.* (Judentum und Umwelt, 26). Frankfurt am Main: Peter Lang.

Díaz Esteban, F. 1968. "References to Ben Asher and Ben Naftali in the *Massora Magna* Written in the Margins of MS Leningrad B19A." *Textus* 6:62-74

Díez Macho, Alehandro. 1965. Magister-Minister. Prof. P. E. Kahle through twelve years of correspondence." In *Recent progress in biblical scholarship*, pp.13-61. Oxford :Lincombe Lodge Research Library.

Diez Macho, Alejandro. 1971. *Manuscritos hebreos y arameos de la Biblia.* Rome: Institutum Patristicum "Augustinianum"

Dotan, Aron. 1976. "Concerning This Edition." [in Hebrew; English in one printing] *The Holy Scriptures.* Tel-Aviv/Ramat-Gan: "Adi"/ Bar-Ilan U.

Dotan, Aron. 1977. *Thesaurus of the Tiberian Masorah. Sample Volume: The Masorah of the Book of Genesis in the Leningrad Codex.* Tel Aviv: Tel Aviv U.

Dotan, Aron. 1989. "Studies in the Massorah of the Leningrad Manuscript." In *Studies in the Hebrew Language and the Talmudic Literature, Dedicated to the Memory of Dr. Menahem Moreshet*, M. Z. Kaddari, et al., eds., pp. 75-82. Ramat Gan: Bar-Ilan U.

Dotan, Aron. 1990. "Masoretic Rubrics of Indicated Origin in Codex Leningrad (B19a)." *VIII International Congress of the International Organization for Masoretic Studies: Chicago 1988*, E. J. Revell, editor. Atlanta: Scholars Press.

Edelmann, R. 1968. "Soferim -- Massoretes, "Massoretes" -- Nakadanim." In *In Memoriam Paul Kahle*, Matthew Black and Georg Fohrer, eds., pp. 116-123. Berlin: Alfred Töpelmann.

Fernández Tejero, Emilia, and María Teresa Ortega Monasterio. 1981. "Las masoras de A, C y L en el libro de Nahum." *Sefarad* 41:27-69.

Fernández Tejero, Emilia, and María Teresa Ortega Monasterio. 1981. "Las masoras de A, C y L en el libro de Joel." In *Estudios Masoreticos (V Congreso de la IOMS)*, Emilia Fernández Tejero, editor, pp. 205-242. Madrid: Instituto "Arias Montano."

Goshen-Gottstein, Moshe. 1962. "Biblical Manuscripts in the United States." *Textus* 2:28-59

Harviainen, Tapani. 1991. "Abraham Firkowitsch, Karaites in Hit, and the Provenance of Karaite Transcriptions of the Biblical Hebrew Texts into Arabic Scripts." *Folia Orientalia* 28:179-191.

Kahle, Paul. 1913. *Masoreten des Ostens: Die ältesten punktierten Handschriften des Alten Testaments und der Targume*. Leipzig: Hinrichs.

Kahle, Paul. 1927. *Masoreten des Westens: I*. Stuttgart: Kohlhammer.

Narkiss, Bezalel. 1990. *Illuminations from Hebrew Bibles of Leningrad*. Jerusalem: Bialik/Ben-Zvi.

Ognibieni, Bruno. 1989. *Tradizioni orali di lettura e testo ebraico della Bibbia: Studia dei diciassette ketiv al / qere wl*. Fribourg: Éditiona Universitaires. 291pp.

Ortega Monasterio, Maria Teresa. 1986. "Las masoras de A, C y L en el libro de Habacuc." *Henoch* 8:149-184.

Perez Castro, F. 1955. "Corregido y correcto el Ms. B19a (Leningrado) frente al Ms. Or. 4445 (Londres) y al Códice de los Profetas de El Cairo." *Sefarad* 15:3-30

Perez Castro, F. 1978. "Una copia del *Codex Hilleli* colacionada con la primera mano del Ms.B19A de Leningrado." *Sefarad* 38:13-24.

Rubinstein, A. 1961. "Singularities in the Massorah of the Leningrad Codex (B19A)." *Journal of Jewish Studies* 12:123-131.

Rubinstein, A. 1965. "The Problem of Errors in the Massorah Parva of Codex B19a." *Sefarad* 25:16-26.

Starkova, K. B. 1975. "Les manuscrits de la collection Firkovic conservés à la Bibliothèque publique d'État Saltykov-Šcedrin." *Revue des Études juives* 134:101-117.

Strack, Hermann L. 1876. *A. Firkowitsch und seine Entdeckungen. Ein Grabstein den hebräischen Grabinschriften der Krim.* Leipzig: J. C. Hinrich s.

Strack, Hermann. 1880. "Abraham Firkowitsch und der Werth seiner Entdeckungen." *ZDMG* :163-168.

Szyszman, S. 1975. "Centenaire de la mort de Firkowicz." In *Congress Volume, Edinbrugh 1974* (Supplements to Vetus Testamentum, 28), pp.196-216. Leiden: E. J. Brill.

Weil, Gérard E. 1981. "Le décomptes de versets, mots et lettres du Pentateuque selon le manuscrit B 19a de Léningrad." In *Mélanges D. Barthélemy*, pp. 651-703. (OBO, 38). Fribourg/Göttingen: .

Weil, Gérard E., P. Rivière and M. Serfaty. 1978. *Concordance de la cantilation du Pentateuque et des cinq Megillot.* [Paris]: Éditions du C.N.R.S.

Weil, Gérard E., and M. Serfaty. 1982. *Concordance de la cantilation des premiers prophetes Josue, Juges, Samuel et Rois.* [Paris]: Éditions du C.N.R.S.

Yeivin, Israel. 1968. *The Aleppo codex of the Bible: a study of its vocalization and accentuation.* Jerusalem: Magnes. [in Hebrew]. Pp. 89-277; xix-xxiii [English summary]

Yeivin, Israel. 1969. "The New Edition of the Biblia Hebraica -- Its Text and Massorah." *Textus* 7:114-123

Yeivin, Israel. 1980. *Introduction to the Tiberain Masorah.* Missoula: Scholars Press for IOMS.

Yeivin, Israel. 1993. "A Biblical Manuscript very close to the Aleppo Codex from the Karaite Synagogue in Cairo (C1)." [in Hebrew] In *Studies in Bible and Exegesis, Vol. III: Moshe Goshen-Gottstein -- In Memoriam*, Moshe Bar-Asher, et al., editors, pp.169-194. Ramat Gan: Bar-Ilan U.

# Michel SERFATY

### Projet Bomberg
Universités Nancy 2 et Pierre et Marie Curie - Paris VI

# UN GUIDE MASSORETIQUE DE PONCTUATEUR :

## LE FRAGMENT : TS-NS 287-21

*A Albert et Laura ATTIAS*
*en affectueux hommage*

Découverts dans la collection Taylor Schechter de Cambridge, les deux folios cités ci-dessous ont appartenu à un même cahier de *Massorah*. Leur examen minutieux révèle qu'ils présentent les mêmes caractéristiques et tout concours à les considérer comme étant écrits de la même main et provenant de la même œuvre. La description qui suit rapportera les aspects paléographiques et scripturaires qui ne laissent aucun doute quant à cette conclusion.

Copiés sur du velin, les deux fragments sont les folios gauches de leurs diplomes d'origine. Ils conservent la *Massorah* en deux colonnes de 29 lignes chacune, suivant une écriture carrée de petite taille mais régulière. On y rencontre des voyelles et des accents de cantilation tibérienne. Les fragments mesurent 23,5 cm X 19,5 cm. Les 29 lignes de chaque colonne occuppent 18,5 cm X 6,5 cm.

TS-NS 287 - 21

La *Massorah* des livres Osée, Joël et Amos jusqu'à 3,5 [1]

Le titre du folio : תרי עשרה, annonce le début de la *Massorah* du livre des Douze Petits Prophètes. Il commence à : [ב] באري Osée 1,1 et finit à : כאדמה ב 11,8 et le folio b continue à : ולא איש ב 11,9 et finit à : [] התפל Amos 3,5.

TS-NS 176 - 11

La *Massorah* de 1 Chroniques 8,6 à 12,8

Le folio a débute à : יעואל ל ומל 1Chr. 8,6 et finit à : ל ויועאלה 1Chr. 12,8 et le folio b continue à : ל למצד 12,9 pour finir à : ולרגל הארץ 19,3.

Au stade actuel de notre reflexion sur les anciennes œuvres de *Massorah*, l'étude de ce fragment pousse à croire en l'existence de catalogues d'un autre genre que celui que l'on connaît sous le nom de'*Okhlah we-'Okhlah*. Les deux folios mentionnés ci-dessus en sont des représentants remarquables. Le but de ces catalogues était de servir de guide au copiste de la *Massorah* qui se voyait confier la ponctuation du texte biblique d'un manuscrit et la notation de sa *Massorah* dans les colonnes verticales aussi bien que dans les marges latérales, en haut et en bas des folios. Dans le cas présent, le travail du copiste qui est vraisemblablement un *naqdan*, consistait à suivre le cahier de *Massorah*, de s'arrêter sur le premier mot de ce guide puis de le rechercher dans le texte biblique et de noter au-dessus de lui un circellus. Puis il portait sa plume vers la marge et recopiait la suite de la note à partir du guide. Puis il passait au mot suivant du guide qu'il lisait et allait le repèrer dans le texte biblique pour le munir de ses voyelles et de sa *Massorah* et ainsi de suite.

Quand la note était courte, il la copiait sur une marge verticale ; quand elle était détaillée, c'est-à-dire, accompagnée des mots-références de sa liste, il la copiait sur les marges latérales du haut ou du bas du folio. C'est encore le guide qui lui indique de laisser tel mot défectif ou de noter après tel autre le *paseq* alors qu'aucune Mp ne signale ces aspects en ces endroits. Arrivant à la fin du livre, le guide lui foournit jusqu'au décompte des versets qu'il notait pour chaque livre, à la fin de son texte. Habituellement, on rencontre l'expression ... סכום פסוקים שלספר , dans le cas présent, chacun des livres est appelé *megillah* -

rouleau, d'un usage plutôt rare sauf à l'époque rabbinique, pour désigner les livres de la Bible. N'est-ce pas là une influence orientale ?

A la fin de cette étude, seul le fragment TS-NS 287 - 21, donnant la *Massorah* des livres Osée, Joël et Amos jusqu'à 3,5 fait l'objet d'une publication détaillée. Son matériel est assez représentatif pour servir de description de ce cahier. Organisé en deux colonnes par folio, le matériel conservé respecte une certaine régularité. Chaque colonne rapporte en moyenne 80 notes de *Massorah*. Le décompte réalisé sur les deux pages révèle au total 317 notes dont 19 de *Massorah Magna* (Mm). En comparaison avec le total des notes de Mp et de Mm du codex d'Alep on observe les résultats suivants :

|  | Mp | Mm | Total |
|---|---|---|---|
| TS-NS 287 - 21 | 298 | 19 | 317 |
| ALEP | 578 | 77 | 655 |
| % de TS / Alep | 51,55 | 24,67 | 48,39 |

L'étude détaillée des notes du fragment par rapport à celles d'Alep, laisse apparaitre un "volume" de matériel bien moins important dans le fragment que dans Alep. Le nombre d'hapax est de 151 par rapport à 286 ; celui des notes quantitatives de 2 à 9 oc. est de 115 par rapport à 194 ; des notes relatives à des expressions ou des successions de mots ou de successions d'accents est de 10 par rapport à 60. Les quantités basses des données de ce fragment peuvent être interprétées diversemment.

On peut reprendre l'hypothèse avancée en 1987 [2] selon laquelle les notes signalant les expressions et les successions de mots ou d'accents sont tardives et qu'elles ont été répertoriées plus tard que les autres catégories de notes. Étalée dans le temps, la constitution progressive de la *Massorah* confirme l'existence de cahiers plus anciens dont on aurait continué à recopier le contenu sans les modifier ni les enrichir de nouveaux apports. Dans le même temps, on continuait de repérer de nouvelles formes hapaxes conduisant à des quantités plus élevées que dans les premiers cahiers. Le présent fragment comporte d'ailleurs des corrections marginales témoignant de l'intérêt que lui portait son propriétaire et sans doute prises de cahiers plus récents et plus riches. En somme, l'analyse de sa *Massorah* autorise à retenir l'hypothèse de l'antiquité de ses listes.

Les commentaires donnés à la fin de ce travail ont permis de tenter de situer ce fragment par rapport à la *Massorah* des trois codex : Alep (A), le Caire (C) et le B19a de Léningrad (L). La statitstique des points communs et des divergences entre les quatre sources textuelles massorétiques fournit les résultats suivants :

| TS=ACL | TS=A | TS=AC | TS=AL | TS=C | TS=CL | TS=L | TS=ø | TS≠ |
|---|---|---|---|---|---|---|---|---|
| 147 | 12 | 52 | 25 | 16 | 7 | 5 | 20 | 12 |
| % : 49,66 | 4 | 17,33 | 8,33 | 5,40 | 2,36 | 1,68 | 7,09 | 4 |

**Légende :**
TS=ACL : leçon du fragment identique à celle des 3 mss.
TS = ø : leçon inconnue dans les codex; seul le fragment la rapporte.
TS = ≠ : leçon du fragment différente de celles des mss.

On reconnait tout d'abord l'appartenance de ce fragment à l'école de Tibériade par le pourcentage élevé des leçons communes au fragment et aux trois mss.. Il présente néanmoins des tendances de parenté plus prononcées vers C (16 leçons communes) et vers A (12 leçons communes) puis vers leurs leçons réunies (52 + 16 + 12 = 80). Il comporte des Mm données aux mêmes endroits du texte que C ce qui l'en rapproche plus que de A. On relèvera surtout le fait particulier qu'il conserve des leçons originales (20 leçons) qui font de lui le représentant d'une tendance intéressante à l'intérieur de la grande famille des œuvres de la *Massorah* de Tibériade. L'une des leçons, p. 3 l. 2, semble entrevoir une proximité avec la *Massorah* orientale. Enfin, on ne manquera pas de préciser une fois de plus et la preuve en est faite ici, que les copistes de A, de C et de L ont utilisé des cahiers de *Massorah* différents.

S'agissant des mots-références des listes de sa Mm on constate une certaine régularité : c'est toujours le premier mot débutant le verset qui sert de mot-référence. Lorsque le verset commence par un nom divin, c'est le deuxième mot du verset qui sert de mot-référence. Ainsi par exemple, dans la Mm de (Jl 4,16) מציון (Ps. 46,2) לנו (Ps. 62,9) בטחו (Jl 4,16) ג מחסה , les deux derniers mots-références viennent dans le verset en deuxième place après des noms divins.

Travail de synthèse, ce type d'œuvre a fait l'objet de copies successives puisque l'on y rencontre des inversions et des interpollations. Les cahiers étaient diffusés en nombre relativement important. Le commerce du codex et particulièrement du codex biblique, ayant pris de l'ampleur, un tel outil massorétique était devenu indispensable. Les copistes ont alors éprouvé le besoin d'avoir à leur disposition immédiate des œuvres - outils massorétiques prêts à l'usage. Ce sont donc ces ouvrages, donnant la *Massorah* de toute la Bible en entier ou partiellement, qui se sont multipliés à leur tour et dont on a perdu les originaux. La conséquence de cette prolifération ne manqua pas de se traduire directement sur les codex, leurs textes et leur *Massorah*. Il ne serait donc pas exagéré de dire que chaque codex pouvait refléter un cahier-guide et qu'à partir de là, un copiste pouvait réaliser un ou plusieurs codex en recopiant le même cahier-guide. Une telle perspective n'exclut pas cependant le cas de figure du copiste avisé ou savant utilisant deux cahiers afin d'enrichir ou d'améliorer la *Massorah* de son codex. La confrontation de différents cahiers-guides devaient également favoriser l'évolution de cet outil pour donner naissance à des cahiers plus denses et plus fournis que notre fragment et se rapprochant des cahiers ultérieurs plus tardifs.

De tous temps, la volonté d'améliorer la *Massorah* et son matériel a été une préoccupation constante des spécialistes de cette discipline. Ils ne manquaient pas de l'exprimer dans leurs écrits. Ainsi par exemple, dans la déclaration introductive de cette œuvre dont il ne nous reste que le fragment TS D1 20, l'auteur écrit qu'il n'a pas trouvé ce qu'il cherchait ni dans la *Grande Massorah* ni dans la *Petite Massorah*, ni dans la *Massorah* Babylonienne, ni dans la *Massorah* Palestinienne, ni dans les œuvres des *Sopherim*. [3] Dans cet autre fragment TS D1 32 il est encore précisé dans le même ordre d'idée : ... ולא מסרו ... בשני לשנין. ‎ במסורת הגדולה ולא במסורת הקטנה, הן בשני לשנין ... . Dans les fragments TS D1-22 (Nb 28 à la fin) et D1-26 (Gn 13,9 à 33,14), deux diplômes d'anciens cahiers-guides de *Massorah* plus tardifs, (dans le D1-26 pour aider le copiste à se repérer dans le manuel, le nom de la péricope hébdomadaire וישלח est noté sur la marge) on reconnait les corrections visant à améliorer le matériel massorétique

A la lumière de cette reflexion, on peut considérer qu'un nouvel axe de recherche s'ouvre aux spécialistes de la *Massorah* et de son histoire. Le désir des chercheurs de notre génération étant de connaître davantage les *Massorah* des grands codex, le nouvel axe consisterait à retrouver le plus grand nombre de cahiers et sur la base de leurs textes, envisager deux approches :

1°) La comparaison des cahiers-guides entre eux.
2°) Le rapprochement des codex aux cahiers-guides

Ainsi donc, le matériel de ce cahier se présente sous la forme de notes rapportées en succession suivant l'ordre des versets, mêlant des notes de *Mp* (= simples) et des notes détaillées identiques à celles que l'on a pris coutume d'appeler : *Mm*. . Une telle organisation du matériel massorétique conduit à s'interroger sur la terminologie jusque-là utilisée et qui consiste à distinguer *Petite Massorah* et *Grande Massorah*. Ce guide semble révéler l'absence d'une telle distinction et pousse à rechercher le nom véritable de son matériel. L'analyse de ces fragments doit permettre de situer leur matériel dans le mouvement de développement de la *Massorah* et à proposer une nouvelle terminologie pour désigner le matériel massorétique.

En effet, à partir du f° 125 b de la *'Okhlah we-'Okhlah* de

Halle, cette œuvre se poursuit par des notes massorétiques se succédant en vrac mais ordonnées selon la chronologie des versets. Elles sont assez proches dans leur conceptions des fragments cités ci-dessus et que l'on a considérés comme des cahiers-guides de copistes de *Massorah*. Leur organisation est simple : une entrée, un chiffre quantificateur, la qualité grammaticale ou accentuelle, enfin le ou les mot(s)-référence(s). Or, fait troublant mais non moins révélateur, ce type de *Massorah* est précédé du titre :

זו ממסורת קטנה

Cette mention demande une interprétation. Comment peut-on appeler *Massorah Qetanah* un matériel rapportant de longues listes explicitant le libellé de la note par une série de mots-références ? Sachant que le début de l'œuvre de la *'Okhlah we-'Okhlah* est uniquement formé de longues listes massorétiques, on peut soumettre au jugement des spécialistes de cette discipline l'hypothèse suivante : les listes de *Massorah* rencontrées dans les codex autour du texte, ou seulement sur les marges latérales, en haut et en bas des folios n'appartiennent pas à la catégorie appelée jusque-là : *Grande Massorah* !! Parcequ'elles ne sont que la stricte explicitation des *Massorah* des marges verticales, elles forment véritablement la *Massorah Qetanah* ou *Petite Massorah* comme en témoigne le titre de ce folio. Par ailleurs, on peut voir une confirmation de cette thèse dans le nom donné à cette autre œuvre sœur, la *'Okhlah* de Paris, en son début :

בעזרת שכן מעלה
אכתב מסרת הגדולה

La *'Okhlah* est donc appelée *Grande Massorah* tandis que que le cahier-guide du copiste venant à sa suite est appelée *Petite Massorah*, sans faire de distinction entre ce qui est donné en abrégé dans les marges verticales et ce qui est donné sous forme de listes détaillée et explicitées dans les marges supérieures et inférieures des folios. Autrement dit : tout le matériel massorétique des codex directement placé autour et à coté du texte biblique ne serait que de la *Petite Massorah*. Aux spécialistes de juger.

\* \* \* \* \* \* \* \* \* \* \* \*

\* \* \* \* \* \* \* \*

\* \* \* \*

**NOTES :**

(\*) Nous tenons à remercier l'Institut des Microfilms près la Bibliothèque de l'Université Hébraïque de Jérusalem qui nous a facilité l'examen des fragments de la *Genizah* ainsi que la Bibliothèque Universitaire de Cambridge qui nous autorisé à publier ce fragment, en particulier le Dr Stefan C Reif, Directeur de l'Unité de Recherche sur la *Genizah* Collection Taylor-Schechter. Merci à notre ami Pierre Rivière pour l'aide qu'il nous a apportée dans la rédaction de notre commentaire.

(1) Les deux fragments n'ont pas fait l'objet d'une étude systématique à ce jour. Cependant, le premier a été cité mais de manière inexacte quant à son contenu. Cf. I. Yeivin, *Encyc. Bibl.* V, pl. 140, Jérusalem 1971 et son ouvrage *Introduction to the Tiberian Masorah*, p. 127, Jérusalem 1986. Cf. G.E. Weil, "La *Massorah*", *R.E.J.* 131 (1972) p. 18.

(2) Voir notre article sur le fragment TS-NS 287-15, dans *Proceeding of the IXe Congress of IOMS - 1989; Masoretic Studies - 7*, éd. A. Dotan, *S.B.L.* U.S.A. 1992, pp. 117 et 118.

(3) ולא מהנמצא במוסרות גדולה ולא במוסרת (חסר !) קטנה ולא במוסרות בני בבל ולא במוסרות בני ישראל ולא בדברי סופרים ...

**Signes conventionnels et abréviations**

[ ] = reconstitution de texte gratté, tâché ou de morceau déchiré.
< > = complément de texte ou de mot non donné dans le ms.
( ) = correction de texte ou de mot erroné; entourent les références bibliques.
A = Ms. d'Alep, Institut Ben Zvi N° 1

C   = Ms. du Caire sur microfilm ou dans l'éd. P. Castro, Madrid 1979 - 1989.

L   = Ms. B19a de Saint Petersbourg.

BgB = *Biblia Rabbinica*, Vénise 1524-25, éd. Bomberg repr. + Intr. M. Goshen-Gottstein Jérusalem 1972

BgM = *Massorah Finalis* de Jacob Hayyim ibn Adoniyah, dans *Biblia Rabbinica*, Vénise 1524-25, éd Bomberg.

GsB = *Bible*, éd C.D. Ginsburg, Londres, 1926.

GsM = *Massorah*, éd. Ginsburg, Londres, 1897-1905.

BHK = *Biblia Hebraica* Kittel-Kahle 4éd.

BHS = *Biblia Hebraica Stuttgartensia*, éd. K. Elliger et W. Rudolph, 1967-83.

MG  = G.E. Weil, *Massorah Gedolah*, Rome 1971.

Mdk = Salomon Mandelkern, *Veteris Testamenti Concordantiae*, 8e éd., Jérusalem 1969.

K-Q = *Ketiv - Qerei*

oc. = occurrence(s)

ø   = Rien en cet endroit dans tel manuscrit.

\*\*\*\*\*\*\*\*\*\*\*\*\*\*\*\*\*\*

## Fragment T-S-NS 287-21

### f° a col. intérieure = p. 1

והארץ ח ר פ (Os. 2,24)

תרי עשרה 1

באריֹ [ב] (Os 1,1) : [ז]ונה ל (1,2) : דבלים ל (1,3) : ממלכות ד (1,4) : [והושעתים ؟] 2

ל (Os 1,7) : ובמלחמה גֹ (1,7) : במסות (Dt 4,34) בקשתֹ)(Os 1,7 מידי חרב (Jb 5,20) 3
[וֹתסר]:

ל (Os 2,4) : כיום יֹ (2,5) : ושתה כת תיה ק (id.) : כארץ ה (id.) : ארחם (2,6) 4

י[וֹא אתֹנֹ פֹת בֹס ארחם)(Os 2,6 עדן (Am. 1,5) הנופלת (Am 9,11) בספרד (Ob 1,20) 5

[ר]שע (Mi 6,11) יוחֹ [האֹזכֹה]י (Mi 6,10) י[וֹ]חיתן (Hb 2,17) לֹ[עד] (So 3,8) לעבדהם 6
תבצענה (Zc 2,13) (Zc. 4,9)

[תשכבנה (Zc 14,2) : צמרי [ ב ] (Os 2,7) : ושקויי ל (2,7) : שֹד לֹ (2,8) : בסיריים 7

לֹ (2,8) : [גֹדרה לֹ (id.) : ורדפה לֹ (2,9) : וב[קשתם ל (id.) : צמרי ופשתי 8

ב (2,11) : ועתה יח [בטעם (2,12) : א ]גֹלה ב (2,12) : חֹנה לֹ (2,13) : חדשה לֹ (id.) : 9

ושבתה ל (id.) : [מו]עדה ל (id.) : אתנה ל (2,14) : ואכלתם ב (id.) : 10

[ו]תֹעד לֹ (2,15) : וחליתה ל (id.) : מפתיה ל (2,16) : וכיום ל (2,17) : 11

[א]שבור בֹ מֹל (2,20) : והלכתיה חסֹ (2,16) : והשכבתים ל (2,20) : 12

וזרעתיה לֹ (2,25) : אהב ל (3,1) : אהבת ל (id.) : כאהבת ל (id.) : 13

ואכרה לֹ (3,2) : ולתך לֹ (id.) : תהיי לֹ (3,3) : ישבו [כֹ ] (3,4) : שר בֹ (3,4) : 14

טובו גֹ (3,5) : אלה לֹ (4,2) : וכחש בֹ (id.) : ודמיתי ל (4,5) : ודמים 15

בֹ (4,2) : [וא]מֹאסאֹך לֹא קֹ אֹ (4,6) : מכהן בֹ (id.) : כרבם ל (4,7) : 16

גֹ אֹמיר בֹ [ (id.) : כעם ככהן בֹ (4,9) : ומקלו לֹ (4,12) : ולבנה לֹ (4,13) : 17

בֹ צֹלה בֹ (id.) : תנֹ)אפנה יֹבֹ סֹו פֹת בסֹ[פרא [ בֹ (id.) : אפקוד גֹ (4,14) : 18

מֹל יפֹרֹדו לֹ (4,14) : וֹעם גֹ (id.) : זנה בֹ (4,15) : כפֹלֹה לֹ (4,16) : [סֹררה ל] (id.) : 19

סֹורר גֹ[ (id.) : יֹו<י>רֹעם גֹ (id.) : ככבש [ בֹ] (id.) : ] 20

] הֹ[בו ל] (4,17) : ] מֹזֹ [בחותם] ל (id.) ] 21

רֹ [צוֹץ ל (5,11) : כעֹש גֹ (5,12) : לר[פא 22

[ בֹ אֹ מֹל וא[ חֹס (5,13) : ] ישחרנני בֹ (5,15) : יֹדֹ לֹ (6,1) : 23

ונד[עה בֹ] (6,3) : כשחר בֹ (id.) : ויבוא 24

[ שכמה גֹ (6,9) : בבית (id.) [בֹ מֹל] 25

שע[רֹו]רֹי[ה קֹ לֹ (6,10) : שת דֹ (6,11) : [ישראל ל (6,10) : 26

] כרפאי לֹ (7,1) : ורעות גֹ (id.) : 27

] אפה לֹ (7,4) : 28

] כתנור גֹ (7,7) : 29

## Fragment T-S-NS 287-21

## f° a col. extérieure = p. 2

1 ‏הפוכה ל (7,8) : כיונה ב (7,11) : פותה ג (id.) : כעוף [השמים]

2 ‏ל (7,12) : כשמע ב (id.) : ממני נֹ (7,13) : משכ [בותם ד] (7,14) :

3 ‏על בָ (7,16) : זו י ב כֹת זו (id.) : שפר טֹ (8,1) : [ידעונך ]

4 ‏ל (8,2) : השירו ל כֹ שין (8,4) : יוכלו יא (8,5) [ ] : שבבים ל](8,6)

5 ‏התנו ל (8,9) : יתנו ל (8,10) : מעט י זק (id.) ? [ : מלך ]

6 ‏שרים ל (id.) : אכתוב כת תב [ ] ק (8,12) : רבו כת בֵי ק [(id.)]

7 ‏הבהבי ל (8,13) : ישראל | פס (9,1) [ ] :

8 ‏משפטיך (Ze 3,15) וישמע (Hg 1,12) חזק (Hg 2,4) [ ] [ :

9 ‏גיל ג (Os 9,1) תשמו(ע)(ח) (id.) אלי (Jb 3,22) יגיל (Pv 23,24) : כֹעמים ל (id.) : ירעֵם

10 ‏גרן (id.) כפרה (Os 4,16) כצאן (Ps 49,15) : לייֹיֹ | פס (9,4) : חג יֹי ] ד (9,5)[

11 ‏השלם ל (9,7) : ידעו יֹאֹ (id.) : ורבה ד אגר[שנו (Ex 23,29) העזובה (Is 6,12)[

12 ‏ב מ משטמה (Os 9,7) רעה (Ec 6,1) : יקוש ל (Os 9,8) :מ[שטמה ב (id.) : יזכור ל מל (9,9) :[

13 ‏יפקוד ל מל (9,9) : כבכורה ל (9,10) : אבותיכם ג [מל בֹס (id.) : כענבים (id.) [

14 ‏קצף יֹי (Zc 1,2) (מ)(ה<)לעולם (Zc 1,5) : וינזרו ל (9,10) : לבשת ב (id.) :כעוף ל (9,11) :

15 ‏ומהריון ל (id.) : בשורי ל כת שין (9,12) : משכיל ב (9,14) : אוס[ף](ג (9,15) :

16 ‏הכה ג (9,16) המוכה (Nb 25,14) שרשם (Os 9,16) כעשב (Ps 102,5) :בלי ב בל ק (Os

: id.)

17 ‏ויהיו יֹאֹ (9,17) : בוקק ב (10,1) : כרב (ד)(זֹ) (id.) : כטוב ד (id.) : יערף ב <)(Os 10,2)

18 ‏ישדד ל (id.) : כרת (10,4) : ל וחסֹ וחד וכרֹת עמו (Nh 9,8) ל ו [?] :

19 ‏כראש ל (Os 10,4) : שכן לֶ (10,5) : אבל ג (id.) : אמללה (Is 33,9) : תירוש (Is 24,7)

20 ‏עליו (Os 10,5) : וכמריו ל (id.) : למלך כֹט (10,6) : בשנה ל (id.) : יקח גָ (id.) :

21 ‏נדמה ל (Os 10,7) : כקצף ל (10,8) : ונשמדו (id.) : כֹו פסו מפקין

22 ‏אלפביתה : כסונו ל (id.) : נפלו ל (id.) : עלוה ג (10,9) : ואסרם

23 ‏ל (10,10) : חֹטאתֹ ל (10,9) : באותי ל (10,10) : ואספו בֹ (id.) : עינתם כת

24 ‏עונֹ קֹ ול כוֹ (id.) : ואפרים (10,11) הֹ וכל מנשה ואפרים כוֹ :

25 ‏מלמדה בֹ (id.) : אהבתי ל (id.) : לדוש ל (id.) : טוב יֹט (id.) : ישדד גֹ (id.) :

26 ‏חרשתם ב (10,13) : וקאם ל קֹר אלף (10,14) : יושד ל (id.) : בשחר ל (10,15) :

27 ‏נדמה כת מוֹ קֹ ול כוֹ (id.) : תרגלתי ל (11,3) : קחם ל (id.) :

28 ‏וממצרים בֹ (11,1) : רפאתים ל (11,3) : בחבלי בֹ (11,4) : בעבתות

29 ‏ל (id.) : ואט ל (id.) : [אוכ]יל ל (id.) : תלואים בֹ (11,7) : כאדמה בֹ (11,8) :

## Fragment   T-S-NS 287-21

### f° b, col. extérieure = p. 3

| | |
|---|---|
| 1 | ] נכמרו [ ג (11,8) : ולא איש ב (11,9) : ויחרדו ל (11,10) : |
| 2 | ] וכיונה [ ל (11,11) : קדושים ב מל (12,1) : ורדף |
| 3 | ]ג ולפקד [ ל (12,3) : ישיב כד (12,3) : בבטן ג (12,4) : וישר |
| 4 | ]ג ויכל ל זק קמ (12,5) : אלהי הצבאות |
| 5 | ]ה [ אהב ט (12,8) : עד יד חס (12,10) : |
| 6 | ] באה]לים ? ב (id.) : אדמה (12,11) ב מה (Lm 2,13) |
| 7 | ] וכעשן ל (13,3) : מארבה ל (id.) : |
| 8 | ] תדע ל זק[ף קמ (13,4) : תלאבות ל (13,5) : |
| 9 | ] וי]רם ב (13,6) : כנמר ל (13,7) : על דרך |
| 10 | ] ? ה (id.) : אשור ל (id.) : ואקרע ל (13,8) : ואכלם ל (id.) : שחתך |
| 11 | ]ל (13,9) : ואקח ל (13,11) : אפרים ח קמ (13,12) : |
| 12 | ] צרור ל (id.) : צפונה ל (id.) : קטבך |
| 13 | ]ל (13,14) : נ]חם] ל [ : (id.) : ישסה ? ל (id.) : יפריא ג (13,15) : והיר>יותיו ל (14,1): |
| 14 | נרכב בָ (14,4) : ירחם ב (id.) : משובתם ל (14,5) : אהבם |
| 15 | ל (id.) : כשושנה ל (14,6) : ויך ל (id.) : כלבנון ד (id.) : ינקתיו |
| 16 | כת (14,7) : כלבנון ד (id.) : ישבו (14,8) ב חס המה (Os 8,13) : יחיו ב (14,8) : |
| 17 | פריך ל (14,9) : ויבן ל בט ג (14,10) |
| 18 | סכום פסוקי המגילה קצ |
| 19 | פתוא/ל ל (Joël 1,1) : ההיתה ל (1,2) : ספרו ל (1,3) : הקיצו ב (1,5) : |
| 20 | חשפה ל (1,7) : אלי ל (1,8) : חגרת ל (id.) : הכרת ל (1,9) : |
| 21 | אדמה יא (1,10) : מן בני (1,12) ד היונה (Lv 1,14) היונה (14,30) ממצרים (Jg 10,11) |
| 22 | הגפן (Jl 1,12) וכ דב ימ כו מן בג ומן בנ]ין ב מ ז |
| 23 | וזעקו ג (1,14) : עבשו ל (1,17) : פרדות ב (id.) : מגרפותיהם |
| 24 | ל (id.) : ממגרות ל (id.) : הביש חס (id.) : נאנחה ב (1,18) : |
| 25 | נבכו ל (id.) : מים ב זק קמ נחליה יבשון (Dt 8,7 et Jl 1,20) : |
| 26 | והריעו ל (2,1) : כשחר ב (2,2) : פרש ב וחס (id.) : נכון (Os 6,3) : |
| 27 | פרש (Jl 2,2) : נהיה ח (id.) : יוסף ד (id.) : בנ]ב יואב (2Sa 24,3) יואב (1Ch 21,3) |
| 28 | עליכם (Ps 115,14) ההרים (Jl 2,2) : כקול י (2,5) : וכפרשים ל (2,4) : |
| 29 | אכלה ה (2,5) : קש ל (id.) : ערוך ]ל (id.) : פא]רור ב (2,6) : |

## Fragment  T-S-NS 287-21

### f° b, col. intérieure = p. 4

1  ‏[כ]גבור]י[ם ב׳ (2,7) : יעבטון ל׳ (.id) : ידח]קון[ ל׳ (2,8):

2  ‏[ יבצעו ל׳ ? ] (. id) ]: וי׳׳י ה׳ בט׳ (2,11) : עשה דב]רו [ ב׳ (.id) :

3  ‏[שבו ] ז׳ חס׳ (2,12) : עם יט׳וכ׳ זק׳כו׳ (2,16) : ולמזבח ב׳ (2,17):

4  ‏ויאמרו ט׳ זקניך (Dt 32,7) נחלו (Jr 16,19) חוסה (Jl 2,17) כולם (Is 14,10) אמת (Is 43,9)

5  ‏תמיד (Ps 35,27) תמיד (Ps 70,5) בגוים (1Chr 16,31) הנו (Jb 38,35) : חוסה ל׳ (2,17):

6  ‏הצפוני ב׳ (2,20) : ותעל ל׳ (.id) : וש]מח[י ל׳ (2,21) : וגפן ל׳ (2,22):

7  ‏ובני-ציון ל׳ (2,23) : הגרנות ]ב[ (2,24):                                    [

8  ‏אשפוך ד׳ מל׳ (3,1) : יחל]מון ל׳ (.id)               ?    בימים ה]המה

9  ‏ח׳ (3,2) : אשפוך ד׳ מל׳ (3,2) : וא]ש ב׳ (3,3) : ]יהפך ב׳ (3,4):

10  ‏לחשך ב׳ (3,4) :בימים ההמה ח׳ (4,1) : ]אש]וב כ׳ י׳ ק[ (.id):

11  ‏והורדתים ל׳ (4,2) : חלקו ל׳ (.id) :ואל עמי ב׳ (4,3):

12  ‏ידו ג׳ (4,3) גורל (.id) נכבדיה (Na 3,10) ירושלים (Ob 11) : בזונה ל׳ (4,3):

13  ‏ו]היל[ד]ה ל׳ (.id) : עלי ל׳ זק׳ קמ׳ (4,4) : לשבאים ל׳ (4,8):

14  ‏ובאו ]ג[ (4,11) : הנחת ל׳ (.id) : ויעלו ג׳ (4,12) : מגל ב׳ (4,13):

15  ‏מחסה (4,16) ג׳ בטחו (Ps 62,9) לנו (Ps 46,2) מציון (Jl 4,16) : והשקה ג׳ (4,18):

16  ‏סכום פסו׳ שלמגלה ע׳ ]ג[

17  ‏בנקדים ל׳ (Am 1,1) : מתקוע ל׳ (.id) : דושם ל׳ (1,3) ]:עדן ד׳ (1,5) חרן [(Ez 27,23)

18  ‏ה׳ ההצ׳׳י׳לו׳ (2R 19,12) ה/הצילו (Is 37,12) : ושברתי (Am 1,5) : קירה ]ב׳ [ (.id):

19  ‏ב׳ ו]השיבותי ל׳ מל׳ (Am 1,8)]: רדפו ל׳ (1,11) : שמר]ה[ ל׳ (.id) ]:

20  ‏]בט׳             הרו]ת ל׳ (1,13) [ :  מאס]ם ל׳ (2,4) : מכרם ג׳ (2,6) :]נעלי]ם(.id) ?

21  ‏]ב׳ (.id) [ : ]השאפי]ם ב׳ (2,6) : וא]יש ואביו [

22  ‏]ענשים ל׳ (2,8) [ : כגבה ]ב[ (2,9) : ואולך ד׳ (2,10) אתכם דוייקרא (Lv 26,13)]

23  ‏אתכם דמשנה תו]רה[ (Dt 29,4) ]אותי דיהושע (Js 24,3) [

24  ‏אתכם דספר ע ]מוס (Am 2,10)         [

25  ‏לנזרים ל׳ (2,11) : ימלט ח׳ (2,11) ואבד (.id) [

26  ‏ותופש (2,15) : ב׳ בו גב ]ר [ (Ps 89,41) ב]חמודו (Jb 20,20) נקי (22,30) רשע (Ec 8,8) [

27  ‏שקר (.Ps 33,17): בגבורים ג׳ (2,16) [                                [

28  ‏היתן ל׳ (3,4) [                                [

29  ‏התפ]ל ל׳ (3,5):                                [

## COMMENTAIRE :

### Folio a col. intérieure = Texte p. 1

Marge supérieure : וʾהארץ חʾ רʾ פ (Gn. 1,2; Lv. 25,23; 26,43; Dt. 11,11; Js. 13,5; Is. 24,5; Ez. 36,34 et Os. 2,24) : Cf. GsM vol. I, lettre *'aleph*, liste 1109 de 8 oc. de ce mot en début de verset, et parmi eux Ez. 36,34 et Os. 2,24. C sur Osée p. 12 donne une Mp חʾ ראʾ פסʾ, seulement sur Os. 2,24. Bg et A rapportent dans Ez. 36,34 et Os. 2,24 la Mp חʾ רʾ פʾ. L Ez. 36,34 חʾ ראʾ פסוʾ et dans Os. 2,24 חʾ ראש פסוק. חʾ ראש פסוק. Cette note n'a pu appartenir aux pages du cahier de la Massorah d'Ézéchiel qui sans doute précédait ce fragment. La référence d'Éz. 36,34 est loin de la fin du livre. Écrite de la même plume qui a servi à noter des corrections ultérieures sur les marges de ce fragment, cette Mp est un ajout que l'on aurait dû trouver au début de la ligne 13, près des notes d'Os. 2,24.

l. 1 : Le titre du livre avec un *he'* final du féminin du chiffre עשר. Cet usage est courant; GsM le signale ; cf. la liste des *Hilluphim* N°606 portant le titre תרי עשרה.

l. 2 זʾ]נה ל // (Gn 26,34) בʾ את יהודית C ; ø L et A (Os 1,1) באריʾ [בʾ]: (1,3) A, דבלים ל // זנו. *qerei* זנה *ketiv* GsB .לʾ וכת הʾ L et C ; .id (1,2) ; בʾ וכל יהושע L .דʾ וכל יהושע A . Mm + .id C (1,4) ממלכות דʾ / / ..id C et L erreur de L , il y a 4 oc. de ce mot (1S 15,28 ; 2S 16,3 ; Jr 26,1 ; Os 1,4) hormis celles de Josué. // [ ? והושעתים] pas dans le fragment. A, C et L לʾ.

l. 3 : גʾ ובמלחמה (1,7) Mm suivie des trois mots-références. A, C et L, Mm avec deux mots-références diférents : ובמופתים (Dt. 4,34) ולא אושיעם (Os. 1,7) מידי חרב (Jb 5,20). A donne une 3e version plus complète, incluant un hapax : או הנסה אלהים (Dt. 4,34) ואת בית ברעב פדך ממות (Jb 5,20) ולא במלחמה וחד באפים (Dn. יהודה (Os. 1,7) 11,20).

l. 4 : יʾ כיום (2,5): Mdk signale 11oc. כיום : Js. 10,13 ; 1Sa. 18,10 ; Is. 9,3 ; Ez. 30,9 ; Os. 2,5 ; Am. 8,10 ; Zc. 14,3 ; Ps. 90,4 et 95,8 ; Lam. 2,7 et 22 ; ainsi qu'une oc. וכיום : Os. 2,17. L semble contenir deux traditions. Sa liste MG N° 1630 sur 1Sa. 18,10 et Am. 8,10 inclut dans les onze oc. וכיום et ignore l'oc. d'Éz. 30;9. Sa Mp conserve 3 fois י, 4 fois יא, une fois ב, Os. 2,5 et 2,17 (= וכיום) et une fois ו, les six oc. du livre des prophètes. (Erreur dans *BHK* qui donne כ) C rapporte une liste différente de 11 oc.; il inclue וכיום et ignore l'oc. de Ez. 30,9. A signale 8 fois 11 oc. et son texte conserve ביום en Ez. 30,9. Notre fragment signale dix oc. et signale en ligne 11 la forme hapax de Os. 2,17 וכיום. Peut-être fait-il allusion à la même leçon que A suivant lequel en Éz. 30,9, il faut lire plutôt : ביום ce qui ramène le nombre d'oc. à 10. // (2,5) ושתה כת תיה ק A, C et L : ושתה et Mp ל וחס. GsB ושתיה. Cas de K-Q inconnu dans R. Gordis, *The Biblical text in the making. A study of the Kethib-Qere*. N.Y. 1937, 1971. // כארץ ה (id.) A et L id.. C a un circellus sur כארץ et pas de Mp sur la marge.

l. 4-6 : ארחם (2,6) וי[א אתנ פת בס] : A, C et L ø. Mm donnant 11 mots dans les Petits Prophètes, portant l'accent *Atnah* sur un *patah* ou sur un *segol*. Texte de A, C, L et Bg אֲרַחֵם. GsB rapporte une divergence אֲרַחֶם dans le ms. 11. La note de ce fragment révèle l'une des divergences vocaliques opposant les maîtres de la *Massorah* de Tibériade. Bg יא פתחי באתנחת. La *Massorah finalis*, (=BgM) d'ibn Adoniyah, lettre *peh*, liste : אלין פתח באתנח וסו פסו תרי עשר בנביא signale 14 cas, 9 avec *atnah* et 5 avec *soph pasuq*. Voir aussi GsM sous *nequdot*, les listes 572-573 et 574. D'une façon générale, les trois listes présentent des divergences notables. La liste 572 est identique à celle d'ibn Adoniyah; la 573 cite 10 oc. au lieu de 11 avec les divergences suivantes : a) ארחם est vocalisé d'un *sereh*, contredisant l'objet de cette *Massorah*. b) Seule l'oc. de Mi 6,10 est citée, celle de 6,11 est omise. c) l'oc. לעבדהם Za 2,13 est omise et remplacée par un K-Q תשגלנה de Za 14,2. Celle du fragment est proche de la 573. Pour la dernière oc. de cette liste, nous proposons Zc 14,2 qui figurait p.e. dans la ligne suivante.

l. 7 : la moitié de la ligne est déchirée. צמרי [ ב (Os 2,6) A, C et L id.. // ושקויי ל (2,7) A, C et L id..// שׂדְ לָ (2,8) A id.. C ל כת ש ; L ø .// בסירים ל(2,8) A et L id. ; C דגל.

l. 8 : וגדרה ל (id.) A, C et L id.. // ורדפה ל (2,9) A, C et L id.. // צמרי ופשתי ב // ה פתחין מיחד. וב[וקשתם ל(id.) A, C et L id.. + Mm de A (2,11), Mp reprenant les deux mots ensemble, venant en plus de la Mp sur chacun de ces deux mots. A et C id. ; L ø .

142 / Michel M. Serfaty

l. 9   : [ בטע ] ועתה יח (2,12), le mot ועתה porte un *tevir*. Le chiffre ה est repoussé vers le bas de la ligne. Bg יח בטע. C יֹ. A et L ø. 18 oc. de ce mot dont עתה de Os. 5,7 avec *tevir*. Cf les références dans l'éd. espagnole de C p. 10. // א[גלה ב... (2,12), Bg לֹ erreur ; C ø ; A et L id.. A Mm (Mi 1,6) ויסדיה (2,12) אגלה ועתה ב. אגלה לֹ // חגה לֹ (2,13) A, C et L id..// לֹ חדשה (id.) A, C et L id..

l. 10   : ושבתה ל ( id.) A, C et L id..// ל מו[עדה[ ( id.) A et C id. ; L ø ./ // אתנה ל (2,14) A, C et L id.. // ב ואכלתם ( id.) A et L id. ; C עצים ב (Jr 5,14).

l. 11   : ו[תעד לֹ (2,15) A, C et L id.. // ל וחליתה ( id.) A, C et L id.. // מפתיה ל(2,16) A et L id. ; C ומל לֹ.// ל וכיום (2,17) A et C id. ; L ø .

l. 12   : א[שבור ב מל], Bg ל מל וח מל בליש ; C ב מל ; A ל מל et Mm (Is. 42,3) ישבור לא תנה רצוץ בלשֹ מל ג (Os. 2,20) אשבור מן הארץ (Jér. 28,12) ;אחרי שבור חנניה L ג מל ; GsM rapporte les trois flexions pleines données par la Mm de A. Ceux qui donnent ce mot hapax font allusion au livre d'Osée. C et notre fragment qui donnent 2 oc., ont p.e. voulu réunir les deux flexions du futur et exclure celle de l'impératif שבור. // והלכתיה חס (2,16), omission du לֹ de cette forme qui devait apparaître dans la ligne précédente. A ל וחס ; Bg et C לֹ ; L ל ל ; // ל והשכבתים ; A et Bg id. ; C et L ø . וחס ו.

l. 13   : de 2,20 à 2,25, le fragment ne signale pas de *Massorah*. // וזרעתיה ל (2,25) Bg, A et C id. ; L ø. אהב ל (3,1) A, C et L id.. // אהבת)ל (id.) A id. ; C וחס ל;L ø. // ל כאהבת ( id.) A, C et L id..

l. 14   : ואכרה ל (3,2) A, C et L id.. // לֹ ולתך (id.) A et C id. ; L ø. // שר בָ //. לֹ תהיי (3,3) A et C id. ; L ø. // ישבו כ (3,4) C et L id. ; A ø . (3,4) ce cas avec *patah* est soit une erreur de copiste, soit un cas unique et original non moins difficile à expliquer. Les grands *codices* le donnent avec *qamas*. C Mm ... וסימנהון ברבות ב au sens de souveraineté. A et L קמ זק ב qui est confirmée par l'en-tête de la Mm de A sur ce mot. Y a-t-il eu confusion avec סַר ? en effet, A et C rapportent à son sujet une Mm סר וזעף (1R. 20,43) וכל סר כתֹ סֹ דכות בר מן ב סַר וזעף(1R. 21,4).

l. 15   : טובו ג (3,5) A et L id. ; Bg et C ומל ג. // ל אֵלֹה (4,2), A et L id. ; Bg et C ה וכת לֹ. GsB signale 3 mss. donnant ק אלוֹ. Cas de mots finissant par une *matres lectionis* ה pour indiquer *holem* et signalés par la note כתֹ ה. // וכחש ב (4,2) A id. ; C et L ø. // ל ודמיתי (4,5), A, C et L id. // ודמים ב (4,2) inversion avec la Mp précédente. C et L id. ; A שפכת ב (1Ch 28,3).

l. 16 : א ק לא 'מאסאך[וא] (4,6), A et L א יתיר ; C א וית[ל. La formulation de notre fragment désigne un *ketiv - qerei.* // ב מכהן (4,6) A, C et L id.. // ל כרבם (4,7) A, C et L id..

l. 17 : la note marginale ג ne semble correspondre à aucun des mots de cette ligne. Peut-être a-t-elle un lien avec le mot נפשו disparu du fait du trou du fragment et dont L rapporte la note : ד דמטעי ג corrigée par Weil en מטעי, et confirmée par GsM, lettre *nun* § 316 p. 284. // ב אמיר[ ג (4,7) C et L id. ; A לשנ בתר ב. // כעם כ ככהן ב (4,9) A et C id. ; L ø. // ל ומקלו (4,12) A, C et L id.. Il existe pourtant une fois avec *waw* et une fois sans *w a w.* // : ל ולבנה (4,13) A et C id. ; L ב reprenant ainsi les 2 oc. avec et sans *w a w.*

l. 18 : ב צ]לה (id.), A et L id. ; C ב כסו (Ps. 80,11). // סו יב תג]אמפנה ב בס]פרא [ פת (id.) A, C et L ø. Liste de 12 mots, dont deux dans Osée, les dix autres dans les XII Petits Prophètes, portant *patah* en fin de verset, pas spécialement sur la syllabe tonique. Voir GsM sous *nequdot*, liste 574 rapportant seulement 11 cas contre 12 signalés par le fragment. Os 4,13 et 5,15 ; Am 9,13 ; Jn 1,6 et 15 ; Mi 7,16 ; Hb 2,3 et 12 ; Zc 3,8 ; 12,4 et 13,4. A, C et L ne signalent pas cette *Massorah* dans aucune de ces références. Voir ci-dessus le commentaire des l. 4-6 sur ארחם/ארחם. // ג אפקוד (4,14) A, C et L ב מל. 2 oc. pleines dont Zc 10, 3. Leçon divergente ou erreur de copiste ? GsB ne rapporte aucune vocalisation divergente dans les 10 oc. de cette flexion. La correction marginale ב מל se rapporte à cette note.

l. 19 : ל יפ]רדו (4,14) A, C et L id.. // ג ו]עם (id.) A et L id. ; C + ב חד מל ; C Mm ; + ב חד חס וחד מל (4,15) L ø ; A ב זנה. //ג. קמ Mm סררה ל [ (4,16) A, C et L id. // ל כפ]רה [ ; Mm + ; Mm + וחד חס ל וחס[ C et A ; L id. (id.).

l. 20 : ג סו]רר(id.) L id. ; A et C ø. // ג יו]רעם[י]ו (id.) L ø ; A et C id. + Mm. // ב [ ככבש (id.) A et L id. ; C ב אלוף (Jr 11,19).

l. 21 : entièrement déchirée ; pas de *Massorah* de 4,16 à 5,11

l. 22 : ל צ]וצ ר (5,11) L ø ; A et C id. // ג כעש (5,12) A, C et L id. // ב בא מל וא חס (5,13) suivant A, C et L. A et L ב חד חס וחד מל ; C ל ר]פא ב

l. 23 : ב ישחרנני (5,15) A et L id. ; C וחס ב (Pv 1,28). // ל יך (6,1) A, C

144 / Michel M. Serfaty

id. ; L ø .

l. 24 : ב ונד[עה (6,3) 2 oc. dans les XII Petits Prophètes dont Jn 1,7; A et L ø ; C ל.// ב כשחר (id.) A, C et L id. + Mm de C . // מל ב ויבוא (6,3) A id. ; L ø ; C Mm de 11 oc. dont 2 pleines.

l. 25 - 26 : ג שכמה (6,9) A et C id. ; L ø . // ל ישראל בבית (6,10) A, C et L id.. // ל ק ה[רו]רו[שע (6,10) note indiquant le K - Q et la forme hapax. A et C id. ; L ק // ד שת (6,11) C id. ; A et L ד.

l. 27 -29 : ל כרפאי (7,1) A et C id. ; L ø . // ג ורעות (id.) A, C et L id.. // ל אפה [מֶ] (7,4) ce cahier ne rapporte pas la particule מֶ. Divergence textuelle ou erreur de copiste ? // ג כתנור [ (7,6 ou 7) C et L id. ; A ø .

**Folio a col. extérieure = Texte p. 2**

Suite de la *Massorah* dans la colonne suivante : Os. 7,7 est suivi de : 7,8.

l. 1 : ל הפוכה (7,8) A, C et L id.. // ב כיונה (7,11) A et L id. ; C ø . // ג פותה(id.) A et L ל ; C ומל ל. Erreur de copiste, ce mot étant hapax ; il serait invraisemblable que cette Mp réunisse les trois participes de cette racine dont deux, Jb. 5,2 et Pv. 20,19 sont au masculin portant des préfixes. // כעוף [השמים] (7,12) A, C et L ø .

l. 2 : ב כשמע (id.) A et L id. ; C צר ב (Is. 23,5) // נֹ ממני (7,13) A, C et L ø ; L n'a pas de Mp de ce mot dans la Torah, ni dans les Psaumes; il conserve en 2Sam. 10,11 יא מ ב דכות תלים וכל נֹ; dans les Hagiographes, il rapporte 8 fois la Mp נֹ; (Job 7,16 ; 13,19 ; 27,5 ; 30,1 ; 42,3 ; Prv. 30,7-18 ; Ecc. 7,23). Ce mot apparaît 88 fois dans la Bible selon le détail suivant : *Torah* 10 oc. + *Prophètes* 29 oc. + *Hagiographes* 18 oc. = 57 oc. (= נֹ) auxquels s'ajoutent 29 oc. des *Psaumes.*// ד בותם] משכ (7,14) A et L id. ; C ø .

l. 3 : ב על (7,16) A et L ø ; C ב et Mm. // זו כת ב י זו (id.) A, C et L ו כת ב ; L rapporte dans Ecc. 7,23 la Mp זה י ב. Ainsi, deux Mp se trouvent réunies dans ce fragments : 2 oc. du démonstratif avec *waw* et 10 oc. avec *he'*.// ט שפר (8,1), A et L מ ב כות אורי וכל חס ג ב; C ט חס ח ; il devait se trouver dans un cahier de *Massorah* une liste donnant un libellé global de 9 oc. réunissant 3 Mp et correspondant à peu près, à la note suivante : חס ג השפר - חס ג שפר חס ג בשפר -. Cf. GsM listes 287, 288 et 289. // ל וידענוך] A, C id.; L ø.

l. 4 : השירו ל כ שין (8,4) A, C et L ש כת ל // יוכלו יא (8,5) A ø ; C et L id.. // [ ל שבבים ] (8,6) A et C id. ; L ø .

l. 5 : התנו ל (8,9) A et C ø ; L id.. // יתנו ל (8,10) A, C et L id. // מעט(id.) A ז ; C et L ; 14 oc. de ce mot portent un *qamas* : 4 avec *soph passuq*, 5 avec *atnah*, 1 avec *revia'* et seulement 4 oc. portent un *zaqeph*. Par conséquent, le ן de la Mp de A, C et L n'indique pas le chiffre 7. Il signifie que ce mot est vocalisé d'un *qamas* et qu'il porte l'accent *zaqeph*. La Mm de MG N° 1208 de L ז קמ וכל אתנח וספ דכות, confime cette interprétation. Quant au *yod* de notre fragment , il reste embarrassant à moins de considérer qu'il désigne les dix oc. avec *soph passuq, atnah* et *revia'*.

l. 6 :[ ל שרים (id.) [מלך] A, C et L rapportent un circellus sur les deux mots alors que le fragment l'utilise seulement sur le 2e mot ; p.e que le premier mot de l'expression se trouvait dans la ligne précédente. // [ק תב כת אכתוב) (8,12) C מל ל; A et L ו יתיר ק אכתב ; // [ורבו כת בי ק : (id.) sur la base de A, C et L.

l. 7-8 : ל הבהבי(8,13) // פס | ישראל (9,1) [ ] משפטיך (Ze. 3,15) וישמע (Hg. 1,12) חזק (Hg. 2,4), note sur les *paseq* des XII Petits Prophètes. Elle apparaît dès la première oc. de cette liste dans le livre. Il n'en est resté que 4 oc. dans le fragment. C signale en Mm sur Hg. 2,4 une liste de 8 oc. de *paseq* et en Hg. 2,12 une Mp לגר déclarant ce cas *legarmeh*. Sans doute il fait allusion à la liste de GsM 142b sous *te'amim*, signalant les 11 cas de *Legarmeh* de ces livres dont cette référence. GsM rapporte 8 oc. dans la liste 212 et signale dans son commentaire, l'existence de listes de 10 oc. dont celle de BgM p. 224, donnant en fait deux cas de *legarmeh*, Hg. 2,12 et Zc. 6,15. La liste de notre fragment garde cependant toute son originalité ; en effet, elle utilise des mots références inconnus à ce jour, dont חזק de Hg. 2,4. Le libellé de cette note ayant disparu, on peut penser, sur la base des longueurs des lignes déchirées, qu'il proposait lui aussi 8 oc..

l. 9 : ג גיל (9,1) גיל ג (id.) אלי (Jb.3,22) יגיל (Pv. 23,24) Mm de 3 oc. ; erreur de copiste sur le 1er mot référence ; L ø ;A et C ג + Mm utilisant un mot référence différent sur les trois : גיל ג וסימנהון וא וגיל גבעות ajoutant (Pv. 23,24) יגיל (Jb.3,22) השמחים (id.) תשמח (9,1) תחגרנה (Ps. 65,13).

l. 10 : ג ירעם (Os. 9,2) גרן (id.) כפרה (Os. 4,16) כצאן (Ps. 49,15) ; Mm

146 / Michel M. Serfaty

de 3 oc. ; A id. ; L ø ; C ד incluant sans doute וירעם (Ps 78,72) // ליויי
פס |(9,4) A, C et L ø . // ד ] יי חג (9,5) A, C et L id. .

l. 11 - 12 : השלם ל (9,7) A et C וחס ל ; L חס ל.ג // יא ידעו (id.) A et C יב ;
L ø ; MG N° 801 12 oc. ; GsM listes 134 ידעו יב, et 135 וידעו יא ; p.e. y
a-t-il eu confusion entre les deux listes. // ד ורבה : אגר]שנו (Ex.
23,29) העזובה (Is. 6,12) משטמה (Os. 9,7) רעה (Ec. 6,1) Mm de 4 oc. ;
A, C et L ד ; + Mm dans A et C donnant des mots-références
différents. // ל יקוש (Os. 9,8) A et L ל ; C ומל ל.// ב ]שטמה מ (id.) A
et L ø ; C וכת ש ב ; la correction marginale ב devait concerner cette
Mp. // מל ל יזכור : (9,9) A, C et L id..

l. 13 - 14 : מל ל יפקוד (9,9) A id. ; C ל ; L ø. // ל כבכורה (9,10) A, C et L
id.. // בס מל ג אבותיכם (id.) כענבים (id.) יי קצף (Zc 1,2) מ)<ה<לעולם)
(Zc 1,5) Mm du fragment. A, C et L ל.// ל וינזרו (9,10) A, C et L ל .
// ב לבשת (id.) A id. ; C ø ; L ל qui semble être une erreur; il en
existe deux : Jr 11,13 et Os 9,10. // ל כעוף (9,11) A et L id. ; C ø .

l. 15 : ל ומהריון (id.) A, C et L id.. // שין כת ל בשורי(9,12) A et L ש כת ל
(9,15) אוס]ף[ ג // . (Jr 50,9) חציו ב C ; .id משכיל ב (9,14) A et L id. ; C ל.// C ;
A מל ל ; C חס ב C ; ג ב ; ל ג ; ainsi les trois notes renseignent l'une sur
l'autre et prouvent leurs différentes origines.

l. 16 : ג הכה)(9,16) המוכה (Nb.25,14) שרשם (Os.9,16) כעשב (Ps.102,5)
Mm du fragment. A ג ; C ג + Mm avec des mots-références
différents ; L ø . // ק בל ב בלי (Os. id.) A קרי בל ; C et L ק בל.

l. 17 : יא ויהיו (9,17) A et L id. ; C יב + Mm de 11 mots-références
contredisant la Mp. // ב בוקק (10,1)A, C et L id.. // <ז)(ד ו)(ז כרב
(Os.9,16) erreur sur ce mot gratté mais assez visible par
confusion avec le mot suivant ; A, C et L signalent avec raison 7
oc. // ד כטוב (id.)A et C id. + Mm de C ; L ø .//<ב ב יער>ף (Os.10,2) la
fin de la ligne est grattée ; A, C, L id..

l. 18 : ל ישדד (id.) A et C id. ; L ø . // כרת : (10,4) עמו וכרות וחד ל
(Nh 9,8) [?] ו ל עמו וכרות. A חס ל ; C et L ל ; + Mm de C donnant
en plus le passif de cette racine וכרות Lv 22,24. Le fragment signale
que l'oc. de Nh 9,8 portant deux fois waw, est aussi hapax. Sur
ce mot, la Mp L וכרות ל est une erreur, seul Os. 10,4 est haser.
Là-bas, les deux mots portent comme sur le fragment, les accents
'azla - geresh.

l. 19 : ל כראש (Os 10,4) A et C id. ; L ø .// ל שכן : (10,5) A et L id. ; C ø
// . ג אבל (id.) אמללה (Is 33,9) תירוש (Is 24,7) עליו (Os 10,5) Mm

donnant en ordre inverse les citations d'Isaie. A et L id. ; C גוחד
ואבל (Am 8,8).

l. 20 : וכמריו ל(id.) A, C et L ø.// למלך כט (10,6) A et L ø ; C id.. // בשנה
ל(id.) A ø ; C et L id.. // יקח גֿ (Os.10,6) sous le *qamas* est notée la
lettre ו indiquant *zaqeph* ; 1Sa 8,11 avec revia' ; Ez 18,8 et Os 10,6.
A, C et L id. + Mm dans C.

l. 21 : נדמה ל (Os 10,7) A id. ; C et L ø.// כקצף ל (id.) C id. ; A et L
ø.// ונשמדו (10,8) כֿו פסו מפקין אלפביתה . כֿו ל ר פֿ Aֿ ; C ø ; L ל ראש פסוק .
Aucun des trois *mss* ne rapporte la Mp du fragment. C donne en
So 3,8 une Mm des vv. contenant tout l'alphabet, y compris les
finales et en Ze 6,11une Mp contenant l'alphabet sans les finales.
Cf. GsM sous *pesuqim* listes 227 signalant 27 vv. dont So 3,8 et
228 signalant seulement le v. de Sophonie. La note du fragment
donnant 26 vv. est donc juste.

l. 22 : כסונו ל (id.) A, C et L id.. // נפלו ל (id.) A, C et L id.. // עלוה גֿ
(10,9) A, C et L id.. // ואסרם ל (10,10)A et C id. ; L ø .

l. 23 : חָטָאת ל (10,9) inversion avec la Mp précédente ; A, C et L ø .
*Merkha'* sous ע.// באותי ל (10,10) A id. ; C et L ø . // ואספו בֿ (id. et
Is 24,22) A, C et L id. // עינתם כת עונ קֿ ול כוֹ (id.) seul le fragment
signale l'hapax avec le K-Q. A, C et L signalent seulement le K-Q
וֹ קֿ.

l. 24 : ואפרים הֿ (10,11) וכל מנשה ואפרים כו ; A et L ø ; C id. jusqu'à la
formulation du collectif, ce qui permet de fonder le lien génétique
entre ce fragment et le cahier de *Massorah* de C.

l. 25 : מלמדה בֿ (id.) A et L id. ; C ø . // אהבתי ל (id.) A, C et L id..//
לדוש ל (id. et 2R 13,7) A, C et L id..// טוב יֿט (id.) A, C et L ø ; Mp
réunissant 12 oc. טוב + 4 oc. בטוב + 1 oc. ובטוב + 2 oc. מטוב = 19 oc..
A et L Mp ל טוב-על le circellus étant sur le *maqqeph*.// ישדד גֿ (id.)
A et C id. ; L ø .

l. 26 : חרשתם בֿ (10,13) A id. ; C בֿ בתר לשנֿ (Jg 14,18) ; L ø . // וקאם ל קֿ :
אלף (10,14) le *lamed* est la particule négative לא, pour dire que le
'aleph n'est pas lu. A et L אֿ כתֿ ל signalent l'hapax et dans ce cas,
le *lamed* indique la particule araméenne לית. C ל. וכתֿ //. ל יושד
(id.) A et L id. ; C ø . // בשחר ל (10,15) A, C et L id. .

l. 27 : נדמה כתֿ מוֿ קֿ ול כו (Os.10,15) A ל ; C et L ø ; indice d'antiquité de
la liste ? en effet, ce cas n'est plus rescencé comme Q-K. // תרגלתי
ל(11,3) A et L id. ; C ø . // קחם ל (id.) A, C et L id..

l. 28 : ב ממצרים (11,1) A, C et L id. . // ל רפאתים (11,3) A id. ; C (Jr

33,6) ל א ארוכה ומרפא ורפאתים ø L ; // ב בחבלי (11,4) A, C et L ø . //

ל בעבתות(id.) A, C et L ø . Inversion des versets 1 et 3.

l. 29 : ל ואט (id.) A et C id. ; L ø .// ל אוכ]יל] (id.) A id. ; C ø ; L ב qui

semble être une erreur, la forme est bien hapaxe. // ב תלואים :

(11,7) A et C ל מל וחד חסר חד ב + Mm de C. L ø .// ב כאדמה (11,8) A, C

et L ל . La forme est bien hapaxe ; erreur dans le fragment ou p.e.

a-t-on voulu inclure (Gn 10,19) ואדמה?

**Folio b col. extérieure = Texte p. 3**

l. 1 : ג [ נכמרו (11,8) A et L id. C ø . // ב ולא איש ב (11,9) A et L id. ; C ב

תולעת ואנכי(Ps 22,7). // ל ויחרדו (11,10) curieuse divergence : texte

de A, C et L וְיחרדו avec *shewa'*.

l. 2 : ל [ וכיונה (11,11) A, C et L ל .// ב מל קדושים ב (12,1) A, C et L מל ג

; L donne une Mm de 3 oc. GM N° 3030 : Os 12,1 ; Ps 16,3 et 2Ch

35,3 et GsM listes N° 44 et 45 cite les mêmes références : P.

Castro les reprend. Pourtant GsB sur Dn 8,24 rapporte des mss et

des éditions, dont BgB, donnant cette oc. pleine. Mdk rapporte 2

oc. pleines sans préfixes : Os 12,1 et Dan 8,24 (L=texte *haser*). En

fait, il s'agit d'une divergence entre orientaux et occidentaux

comme le signale la fin de la note 45 de GsM הלין למערבאי, ולמדנחאי

מוסיפין והשחית עצומים ועם קדושים (Dn 8,24). Le fragment semble

donc conserver une *Massorah* orientale signalant 2 oc., soit les 2

formes non préfixées, soit les 2 oc. préfixées. En tout état de

cause, nous sommes en présence d'un cas de divergence qui

pourrait témoigner de l'antiquité de cette liste, étant la seule à

conserver une liste orientale à l'intérieur d'un cahier occidental.

// ורדף (12,1) A, C et L id. .

l. 3 : ל [ ולפקד (12,3) A, C et L id. . // כד ישיב (12,3) A, C et L ø ; Mdk 26

oc. . // ג בבטן (12,4) A et L ø ; C id. . // ג[ וישר] A, C et L ש כת ג.

l. 4 : קמ זק ל ויכל] (12,5) A et L וחס ; C . ל.// ה הצבאות אלהי (12,6)

A et L id. ; A donne le circellus sur הצבאות et pas entre les deux

mots. C ø .

l. 5 : ט אהב (12,8) A, C et L id. // חס יד עד (12,10) A et C id. ; L חס יב

בעד 2 et עד Mdk 12 .

l. 6 : ב ? באה]לים] (id.), lecture incertaine, le fragment étant gâté ; A

149 / Michel M. Serfaty

et C ד ; Mdk 4 oc. ; curieuse leçon sans doute erronée de L ל כת א .
אדמה (12,10) ב מה (Lm 2,13) A et L ב ; C מה אעידך Lm 2,13. //
l. 7 : וכעשן ל (13,3) A, C et L ø . // מארבה ל (id.) A id. ; C et L ø .
l. 8 : תדע ל זק]ף קמ] six oc. de cette flexion portent *qamas*, dont trois
avec *silluq* (Ez. 38,14; Prv. 30,4; Job 11,8) et deux avec *atnah* (Is.
58,3; Job 38,5). A et C id. ; L ø . // תלאבות ל (13,5) A et C id. ; L ב ;
erreur dans L.
l. 9 : וי]רם ב (13,6) A et L id. ; C כמרעיתם בָ(Os 13,6), כבודם (Ez 10,4).
כנמר ל (13,7) C id. ; A et L ø .// על דרך ה (id.) suivant A et C ; L ד //
l. 10 : אשור ל (id.) A et C ø ; L id. . // ואקרע ל [ (13,8) C et L ø ; A id.
ואכלם ל (id.) A, C et L id. . // ל ] שחתך (13,9) A, C et L id. . //
l. 11 : ואקח ל [(13,11) A, C et L id. .// אפרים ח קמ (13,12) C קמ ד ; A
et L ד אפרים, signalés par un *simman* dans C חוטרא (Nb 13,8)
דמיכיהו (Jg 17,1) צרור (Os 13,12) ומתקן (Os 4,17) sur 46 oc. portant
*qamas*, huit portaient *zaqeph*. (?).
l. 12 : les notes de 13,11 et 12 sont inversées. צרור ל [(id.) A et C id. ;
L ø.// צפונה ל (id.) A, C et L id. . // ל ] קטבך (13,14) suivant A, C et
L .
l. 13 : נ]חם ל (id.) A, C et L id. . / / יפריא ג (13,15) erreur de scribe ;
c'est un hapax. C ל מל ; A et L ל ; ל ? ישסה (id.) A et C id. ; L ø . // :
והר<יותיו ל (14,1) A ø ; C id. ; L donne une Mp ל sans circellus
dans le texte.
l. 14 : נרכב בָ (14,4), ne signale pas *zaqeph*. A id. ; C ועל קל (30,16 ) ;
משובתם ל //;לַ וא קמ C ; יוחם ב (id.) A id. ; בְ זקף קמצ L.// ב זקף קמצ L (14,5) A,
C et L ø . // אהבם ל (id.) A et L id. ; C וחצ ל.
l. 15 : כשושנה ל (14,6)A et L ø ; C וחד כשושנה בין ל (Ct 2,2) // ל (id.) A, C et L id. . // כלבנון ד (id.) A id. ; C et L ø . // ינקתיו כֹת (14,7)
semble indiquer le *qoph haser waw* ; textes de A, C et L *male'*
*waw*. A et L ב ; C ø .
l. 16 : כלבנון ד (id.) A, C et L ø, déjà mentionné dans l'oc.
précédente. // ישבו ב חס (14,8) המה (Os. 8,13) : Il en existe sept
*haser*. Le fragment signale seulement les deux oc. de Osée dont
celle de 8,13 qui est *male'* dansL . // יחיו ב (14,8) A et C ב ואתך (Gn
12,12).
l. 17 : פריך ל (14,9) A et C id. ; L ø . // ל בט ג ויָבֶן (14,10), avec
*munah-qamas* et *sereh ga'ya'*; note rare indiquant les deux

informations : hapax d'accent et 3 oc.. Comme le ג n'est pas suivi des deux points habituels et qu'il est précédé de grattage, il est peut-être un ajout tardif.

l. 18 : Le livre est appelé המגילה - le rouleau. A la fin des notes du livre de Joël, f° b col. int. l. 16, il utilise plutôt שלמגילה.

l. 19 : פתואל ל (Joël 1,1) A, C et L id. . // ל ההיתה (1,2) A, C et L id. ספרו ל // : (1,3) A, C et L id. .// ב הקיצו (1,5) A id. ; C ב ורננו , deux oc. dont Is. 26,19 ; L ל , p.e. pour les XII livres seulement.

l. 20 : חשפה ל (1,7)A et C id. . L ø . // ל אלי (1,8) A, C et L id. . // חגרת(id.) A id. ; C ל וחס;L ø . // ל הכרת (1,9) A et C id. . L ø .

l. 21 - 22 : אדמה יא (1,10) A, C et L id. . // ד מן בני (1,12) היונה (Lv 1,14) וכ דב ימ כו מן בנ ומן בנין] הגפן(Jl 1,12) ממצרים (Jg 10,11) היונה(14,30) ז מ ב ב ; A id. et pas de Mm ; C id. + Mm presque identique à celle du fragment ; cf. les commentaires dans l'éd. de P. Castro.

l. 23 : וזעקו ג (1,14) A et L ג ; C id. . // ל עבשו (1,17) A et C id. . L ø ממגרות ל (id.) : // ל מגרפותיהם (id.) A, C et L id. . // ב פרדות (id.) ./ נאנחה ב (id.)(1,18) ; textes de A, C et L haser. הביש חס

l. 24 : ממגרות ל (id.) A, C et L id. .// הביש חס (id.) A, C et L ø ; dans l'oc. de Jl 1,14, L conserve la note ד מ ב דכות הימ דב וכל (וחס) ד . // נאנחה ב(1,18 et Lm 1,8) A, C et L id. .

l. 25 : נבכו ל (id.) A id. ; C ל וחס ; L ב , erreur de L . // מים ב זק קמ (1,19) suivi de נחליה יבשון , simman faisant allusion aux oc. Dt 8,7 ארץ נחלי מים : et Jl 1,20 : אפיקי מים יבשו et dont il reprend deux mots. A et L זק קמ + Mm de A ... וכל אתנח וסוף פסו ; C ב ז ק + ; נחלייא יבשון Mm utilisant les formes נחלי יבשו ; La formulation araméenne du simman n'est donc pas régulière compte tenu des différences qu'elle présente ailleurs. Cf. MG N° 1097 : נחלייה [וסימן בלשון תרגום] יבישין .

l. 26 : והריעו ל(2,1) A et L id. . // ב כשחר (2,2) A et L id. ; C נכון ב רפ. (Os 6,3) פרש (Jl 2,2). Interpollation de Mm de ב כשחר et de la Mp de ב חס פרש. Par mégarde, le copiste a noté ב חס devant le mot-référence פרש, qui explique la note de ב וחס // כשחר.(id.) A ל וחס ; L ל ; C ø ; ce mot est hapax.

l. 27 - 28 : נהיה ח (id.) A et C ח; L ø . // יוסף ד (id.) בנ יואב (2Sa 24,3) יואב(1Ch 21,3) עליכם (Ps 115,14) ההרים (Jl 2,2) : יוסף quatre oc. de ce mot signalés par un simman sous le groupe בנ = Prophètes, alors que deux d'entre eux sont dans les Hagiographes. A : ד וכל

אור כות ב מ ב (וכל שם אנש דכות). entre parenthèses, un ajout tardif dans A. (Deut. 25,3 : 2 oc. *haser* mais avec *hiriq*). L'éd. P. Castro propose par confusion la référence de Lév 5,16. יוסף ד (id.) בנב יואב (2Sa 24,3) יואב (1Ch 21,3) עליכם(Ps 115,14) ההרים (Jl 2,2) // Inversion des notes de כקול et de וכפרשים : י כקול (2,5) A et C id. ; L ø . // וכפרשים ל (2,4) A, C et L ø .

l. 29 : אכלה ה (2,5) A id. ; C ואכלה ; ה וא ; L ø . // קש ל (id.) A לֹ ; C et L ø.// ל] ערוך (id.) A, C et L id. . // פא[רור ב (2,6) A, C et L id. .

## Folio b col. entérieure = Texte p. 4

l. 1 : ב ם[גבורי]ו[כ] (2,7) A, C et L ø . // יעבטון ל (id.) A, C et L id. . // ל [קון]ידח (2,8) A, C et L id. .

l. 2 : ל יבצעו (id. ) ? A ø ; C et L id. . // ויי ה בט [ (2,11) A ראש בט ו ; ב בטע ו ; L ø . GsM lettre yod N° 198 a trouvé 9 listes donnant 6 oc. du tetragramme en début de verset portant *revia'* : Gn 19,24 ; 1 Ro 5,26 ; Jl 2,11 ; Jn 1,4 ; Jb 42,10 et 12. Mm de L sur Jb 42,10 confirme cette liste, cf. MG N° 3567. GsB signale dans Jn 1,4 des *mss* conservant un *gershayim* et d'autres un *zaqeph gadol* au lieu du *revia'*. Y a-t-il un lien entre eux ? // ב [ דבֹ]רו עשה (id.) A et L id. ; C ב ברכו (Ps 103,20).

l. 3 : חס ז [ ו ]שבו (2,12) : la lecture minutieuse du fragment permet de retenir *zayin* plutôt que *waw*. A et L חס ה, 5 oc.. C ø. En fait il en existe 7 oc. et 1 oc. ושבו *qerei-ketiv* lui aussi *haser* : Gn 43,2 et 44,25 (Mp L מל ג ב מ חס אורית כל : contradictoire; il n'y a dans la Torah que 4 oc. dont Gen 43,13 et Dt 5,27 de vocalisation pleine); IRo 17,13 (Mp L בטע ה ); Is 21,12 (Mp L חס ה ); Jr 35,15; Jo 2,12 (Mp L חס ה ); Job 6,29a et b (Mp L ושבו ק ). Les confusions ont pu naître du mélange des notes בטע ה et חס ה.// כו זק וכ יטֹ עם (2,16) ולמזבח ב // .יז וכל אתנ וסו פסו דכות L ; ב A ; .יט וכל את וסו פס דכות C (2,17) A, C et L id. .

l. 4-5 : ט ויאמרו (id.) A, C et L id. ; A rapporte une Mm avec un ordre identique; L donne une Mm avec un ordre différent. C Mp. // ל חוסה (2,17) A, C et L id. .

l. 6 : ב הצפוני (2,20) A ב + Mm את הצפוני משפחת לצפון לשנין בתר ב ; C ; ב לצפון משפחת (Nb 26,15) ; L id. ; // ל ותעל (id.) A, C et L id. . // ל וגפן (2,22) A לֹ ; C ø ; L id., le ל י[מח]וש (2,21) A, C et L id. . //

circellus est placé entre les deux mots תאנה וגפן .

l. 7 : ובני-ציון ל (2,23) A, C et L id. . // הגרנות ב (2,24) A, C et L id. .

l. 8 : אשפוך ד מל (3,1) A, C et L id. . // יחלמון ל (id.) A et C id. ; L ø . בימים ה[המה A יב le circellus est sur ההמה ; C et L ח. //המה ה[המה ח//

l. 9 : אשפוך ד מל (3,2) A, C et L id. . // ואוש ב (3,3) A בּ ; C ø ; L דם ואש ב ; le circellus concerne les deux mots. // יהפך ב (3,4) A ב ; C ב עליך (Is 60,5) ; L ø .

l. 10 : לחשך ב (3,4) A et C ø ; L ב.// בימים ההמה ח (4,1) A, C et L id. . גכת י ק . ; C אשיב ק ; L ואש[וב כ י ק] (id.) A et L ק// 

l. 11 : והורדתים ל (4,2) A et L ø ; C id. // חלקו ל (id.) A, C et L id. . // ואל עמי ב (4,3) A et C ל ; L ג. On trouve 4 oc. sans w a w devant אל : Gn 49,29 ; Ez 13,19 ; Am 7,15 et 8,2, et une avec w a w: Jl 4,3 . Le ג de L fait p.e. allusion aux trois oc. des Douze petits prophètes. Autre thèse : les Mp de ואל עמי et du mot suivant ידו se sont inversées dans L .

l. 12 : ידו ג (4,3) Mm de 3 oc.. C rapporte au même endroit une Mm donnant des mots-références différents. Erreur dans L qui note ל, cf. ligne précédente. A et C id. . // בזונה ל (4,3) A id. ; C et L ø .

l. 13 : ו[ו]היל[ו]ד[ה ל (id.) A et L id. ; C ל דג.// עלי ל זק קמ (4,4) A ל ; C ל ג ; C לשבאים ל .// ל זקף קמץ L ; ק.

l. 14 : ובאו [גו] (4,11) A et L id. .// הנחת ל (id.) A et C id. ; L ø . // ויעלו מגל ב (4,13) A, C et L id. . // ג(4,12) A, C et L id. .

l. 15 : מחסה ג (4,16) בטחו (Ps. 62,9) לנו (Ps. 46,2) מציון (Jl. 4,16) Mm de 3 oc.. A id. + Mm donnant 3 oc.. C id. + Mm détaillée : חסיון ט רפ ; il בלש מחסה ג מחסי ב לחסות ג חסיה ג חסיה א וסימנ בטחו לנו מציון ... ח בליש L . conserve encore trois Mp : Jl 4,16 ג ; Ps 46,2 ג ; Ps 62,9 בליש ח et Prv 14,26 ח. Cf MG N° 3046 et 3278. La Mm de C permet de comprendre l'objet de la Mp de 3 oc.. La note de L signalant 8 oc. n'est pas une erreur, étant confirmée en d'autres endroits. Elle peut être le regroupement des trois premières notes rapportées par C ; on peut observer mais sans en tirer de conclusion, que sur les 8 oc. de מחסה, 3 d'entre elles ont la lettre *het* vocalisée d'un *hateph patah* tandis que dans les cinq autres, elle est vocalisée d'un *shewa'*.

l. 16 : Total des versets du livre - מגילה - de Joël 73.

l. 17 : *Massorah* du livre d'Amos

l. 17-18 : בנקדים ל (Am 1,1) A, C et L id. . // מתקוע ל (id.) A et L id. ; C

ø . // דושם ל (1,3) A, C et L id. . // עדן (Am. 1,5) Mm de quatre oc.. A

דְ ; L ד et Mm ההצילו (2R. 19,12) ההצילו (Is. 37,12) חרן וכנה (Ez.

27,23) ושברתי (Am. 1,5) Cf Weil N° 3050; C Mm עדן ג וסימנהון ההצילו

ההצילו ושברתי וחד חרן וכנה ועדן. Erreur de copiste de notre fragment
modifiant les deux flexions du passé en l'hébraïcisme hapax ההצל
הצילו (2Rois 18,33) ; une autre main a ajouté la lettre he' entre les
deux lignes, sur le deuxième mot référence.

l. 18 : קירה portetiphha' sous le qoph. L'oc. de 2Rois 16,9 porte
un'atnah. A et L id. ; C ø .

l. 19 : מלי ל] והשיבותי (Am 1,8). A ל מל ב בטע ; C ל מל ל בטע ; ב בטע ; L ø . Sur la
marge du fragment, a été ajoutée en trois lignes, la mention ב בט,
et le signe de l'accent 'azla' sur la lettre bet. Cette note concerne
le mot והשיבותי dont la Mp de A et la Mm de C donnent les deux
notes : ל מלי et ב בטעי. Cet ajout sur la marge confirme l'antiquité
de la note signalant l'hapax conservé dans ce fragment, la note
sur deux oc. accentuées en la lettre bet, étant tardive. L n'a
conservé que cette dernière. C l'a explicitée ainsi : עקרון (Am. 1,8)
(Ez. 20,22) בבית וסימנ ואעש ב בט . // ל רדפו (1,11) A, C et L id. . //
שמר]ה[ ל (id.) A, C et L id. .

l. 20 : הרו]ת ל (1,13) A, C et L id. . // מאס]ם ל [ (2,4) A, C et L id.
(Nb ג וסימנהון ונתתי C de Mm + ; . id L et C ,A (2,6) מכרם ג // .
20,19) בכסף (Am 2,6) ציד (Nh 13,15) . // ב נעלי]ם[: (id.) ? .

l. 21 : Restitution incertaine.

l. 22 : [ ] (2,10) // ד ואולך] [ (2,9) // [ב] כגבה (2,8) // ל ענושים] : ל .

l. 23-24 : Texte déchiré. Les références de la Mm sont celles de [ ]
(Dt 29,4)[ אתכם דמשנה תו]רה[ (Lv 26,13) ]אתכם דויקרא (2,10) ואולך ד]
אותו דיהושע (Js 24,3) [מוס ע אתכם דספר (Os 2,10) A, C et L id. ; +
ד וסימנהון קוממיות Mm de C avec des mots-références différents
ארבעים.

l. 25 - 27 : לנזרים ל (2,11) A, C et L id. . La Mm qui suit a été
reconstituée à partir des trois codices grâce aux deux mots-
référence qui en sont restés : ח ימלט [ (2,11) ואבד (id.) בו ותופש ב]
(2,15) [ ר] גב [ (Ps 89,41) חמודו] ב (Jb 20,20) נקי (22,30) רשע (Ec 8,8)
שקר](Ps. 33,17) // ג בגבורים (2,16) A et L id. ; C ø .

l. 28 - 29 : היתן ל (3,4) A, c et L id. . // [ ל התפ]ל (3,5) A, c et L id. .

# IS TIBERIAN *Səgôl* A PHONEME?

Richard L. Goerwitz
University of Chicago

## 1 Introduction

Close examination of relevant vowel distributions within the Tiberian Hebrew corpus reveals that supposed instances of *ṣērê* : *səgôl* and *səgôl* : *pátaḥ* oppositions reduce mainly to *səgôl*-less /e/ versus /a/ contrasts. Cases where *səgôl* functions as a separate phoneme, /ɛ/, turn up in just a few marginal environments. Given that writing systems tend to ignore marginal phonemes, why is it that the Tiberian scribes made such systematic, aggressive use of a *səgôl* grapheme? My contention here will be that systematic use of the *səgôl* grapheme reflects, not so much the raw vowel distributions observable in the Tiberian Hebrew corpus, as subconscious perceptual mechanisms that the Tiberian scribes acquired through exposure to living languages. The question of whether *səgôl* is a phoneme or not, therefore, hinges not only on the intrinsic structure of the Tiberian dialect, but also, more importantly, on the living languages used by the people who transcribed it.

## 2 What is a Phoneme?

Before delving into the question of *səgôl*'s phonemicity, let me pause briefly to consider the question, "Just what exactly *is* a phoneme?"

According to all of the classic structuralist manifestos — e.g., Saussure, Bloomfield, Trubetzköy — the phoneme is the smallest unit that a language, as a system, can be broken down into. One can turn the /p/ in *pat* into a /b/, for instance, resulting in a new word, *bat*.

155

One can also switch the vowel in *pan* (usually transcribed *æ*) with /ɪ/, resulting in *pin*, or the /t/ in *pat* with /d/, resulting in *pad*. Notice that the /æ/ vowel in *pad* is a little longer than the one in *pat*. This does not mean that the long /æ/ ([æː]) differs systematically from its short counterpart. The fact is that the difference in duration here is totally predictable. And so most English speakers do not even notice it. As a result, they analyze the two *æ* sounds as different realizations, i.e. allophones, of a single linguistic entity, namely the phoneme /æ/.

Though structuralist ideas about the phoneme resulted in many solid, working analyses, linguists within the structuralists' own ranks began to realize that languages could be broken down into even smaller elements than phonemes (Jakobson, 1962). In English, for example, we automatically nasalize an /æ/ if it precedes an /n/ or an /m/. Because /n/ and /m/ share the feature of nasality, it would seem sensible to view this /æ/ → /æ̃/ rule as reflecting not two phonological processes (one for /n/ and another for /m/), but rather just one, namely the backwards spread of /n/ and /m/'s nasality into a preceding vocalic segment. Formal linguists might notate such a rule as: V → V[+nasal] / _[+nasal] (to be read, "A vowel becomes nasalized before a [+nasal] segment"). In fact, not all vowels nasalize this way in all environments, so the above formalization requires further refinement. The point, though, is that, by analyzing down to the level of sub-phonemic traits like nasality, and by bunching these traits together into larger phonemes, structuralists created a new system in which the old atomic units, /n/, /m/, /æ/, etc., gave way to complexes of sub-atomic features. This system allowed terser and more elegant formulations of many phonological processes, such as the nasalization of /æ/ before /n/ and /m/.

Although structuralists themselves originated the notion of phonemes as complex units, this view, ironically, reached the pinnacle of its popularity among generative phonologists. Taking their cue from scholars such as Jakobson, Halle, and Chomsky, generative phonologists worked out a new theory of phonemes as minimally redundant feature matrices that combined to form morphemes, which the syntax, in turn, arranged into sentences — which were, at last, re-formed by the phonology proper into an actual speech stream. In such a scheme, phonemes subsumed only unpredictable traits. Since nasalization and lengthening of /æ/ were predictable in English, [æ̃], [æ̃ː], and [æː] were not underlying phonemes. Rather they derived, by nasalization and lengthening rules, from the minimal binary feature matrix

$$\begin{bmatrix} +vocalic \\ +low \end{bmatrix}$$

Though no longer atomic, like the early structuralist phoneme, such matrices were usually treated, for simplicity's sake, as units — i.e., as so-called systematic phonemes. These systematic phonemes formed the basic building blocks out of which generativists constructed all underlying, lexical forms.

While advances in lexical phonology, metrical phonology, optimality theory, and other areas of theoretical linguistics have certainly modified the insights of the early generative phonologists, the terms and general framework they developed in the 1960s still form the core of phonological theory today (e.g., segmental structure preservation theorems in lexical phonology; Mohanan, 1986:173-181). For lexical phonologists, phonemes are the basic units out of which the abstract morpheme inventory of a language (i.e., its lexicon) is built. In practice, these units are equivalent to the systematic phonemes described above.

## 3    The Distribution of Tiberian *Səgôl*

Interestingly, whether we look at phonemes from a structuralist or a generativist standpoint, we gain largely same insight into *səgôl*, namely, that it was at best a marginal phoneme, and, for the most part, just a synchronic reflex of /e/ or /a/. Take, for example, the verb ʔelékɔ[h], 'I will go' (pausal) and the suffixed preposition, ʔelé[y]kɔ, 'to you (ms)':[1]

אֵלֵכָה : אֵלֶיךָ

Superficially, this word pair might seem to evince a phonemic *ṣērê* : *səgôl* contrast. Notice, though, that we are talking about a two-way distinction. There is no third form with a *pátaḥ* in the stressed syllable:

---

1. On my vowel transliterations, see Johnson and Goerwitz, 1995.

אֵלֶיךָ : אֵלֶכָה : *אֵלָכָה?

Aside from a few well-known exceptions (e.g., [-]CáyiC, 1cs verbal -
ani[y]; Ruth 2:7, 4:15), Pátaḥ simply does not occur in this environment. As the structuralists would put it: pátaḥ in open, stressed syllables stands in complementary distribution with səgôl. This complementary distribution, in addition to their basic phonetic similarity,
constitutes grounds (in the structuralist scheme) for analyzing səgôl and
pátaḥ here as allophones. If səgôl and pátaḥ are allophones, then the
phonological difference between the words ʔelékɔ[h] and ʔelɛ́[y]kɔ,
boils down to a difference between a mid vowel (ṣērê) and a low vowel
(səgôl/pátaḥ). There is no evidence here, then, for a separate səgôl
phoneme.

Though the generative model rests on a somewhat different set of
assumptions, it leads us, in this case, to the same set of conclusions as
the structuralist model. According to the generative model, the
appearance of səgôl (and, conversely, the absence of pátaḥ) in
ʔelɛ́[y]kɔ is predictable (by way of the rule, $a \to \varepsilon$ / _{C[-low]V, #}).
As a result, we need just one phoneme at the lexical level to represent
it.[2] From both generative and structuralist standpoints, therefore, səgôl
is not an underlyingly distinct phonological entity. It is, rather, just
one of several possible surface realizations of the low vowel, /a/.

Note that this reasoning does not apply solely to the two forms
cited above, ʔelékɔ[h] and ʔelɛ́[y]kɔ. Similar reasoning might be
applied to any number of minimal pairs. Compare, for example, cstr.
miqne[h] : abs. miqnɛ[h]; hazze[h] 'cause to sprinkle' : hazzɛ[h]
'(art.)+this'; ḥable[y] (< ḥebɛl 'cord, territory, band') : ḥeblɛ[y] (<
ḥébɛl 'pain, pang'). The səgôl in this last form, ḥeblɛ[y], results from
lowering of an underlying /e/ vowel after ḥet. In other words, səgôl
here is an allophone of /e/, rather than /a/. Whether derivable from /e/
or /a/, however, the point remains the same: səgôl is virtually always
to be analyzed as low-level derivative of some other phoneme.

---

2. Sadly, generative treatments of the language generally assume a length
feature separating /ṣērê/ from /səgôl/ — seemingly unaware that /səgôl/ can be
either short or long (Johnson and Goerwitz, 1995:17).

Even Cantineau's now classic "proof" of *səgôl*'s phonemicity, *ʔal* (negative) : *ʔɛl* 'to' : *ʔel* 'god' (Cantineau, 1950:109) turns out to be re-analyzable into stress-conditioned variations: *ʔɛl* 'to' is proclitic, while *ʔel* 'god' takes full, independent stress.[3] *Səgôl*, then, does not contrast with both *ṣērê* and *pátaḥ* in any one environment because, in each case, it is an allophone of one of these two phonemes (Corré, 1967:65).[4]

The only real flaw in this analysis is that it does not deal well with idiosyncratic forms — i.e., forms in which the appearance of a *səgôl* in place of *ṣērê* or *pátaḥ* cannot be attributed to any low-level phonetic processes. Take, for example, the Hebrew word for 'bread', *léḥɛm*, which takes two *səgôl*s. Compare, now, *náḥal* 'wadi', which takes two *pátaḥ*s. The stressed [ɛ] and [a] in these forms both occur before the guttural *ḥet*. Why, then, do these vowels differ, despite the fact that both forms are historically *\*CaCC*? E. J. Revell has expended a lot of energy showing that segolate vowel patterns interact, not only with the second, but also with the first, root consonant (Revell, 1985). And, because *léḥɛm* and *náḥal*'s initial consonants differ, one might be tempted to treat them as distinct phonological environments. Revell's data, though, are not wholly consistent, and in the end he is forced to conclude that the rules are not hard and fast. In practical terms, this means that unless we posit a lexical or systematic *səgôl* in *léḥɛm*, we have no obvious way of explaining why we get a *səgôl* on the surface as well, since the underlying /a/ here would usually be expected to come out as [aː] before a *ḥet*.

It ought to be pointed out, however, that the CVCVC segolate environment is very late (< earlier *\*CVCC*), and that the distinction

---

3. Cf. Revell, 1970:103 n.10. In three cases the word *ʔel* is proclitic, but the lowering rule, /e/ → [ɛ] does not apply (Ezek 10:5; Pss 86:15, 94:1). This morphophonemic problem also affects words like *leb* and *šem*. It might stem from a clash between vocalic and accentual traditions (regarding which, see Revell, 1976).

4. Note the modern Aramaic dialect of Mangesh, which has [e] and [ɛ] allophones of /e/ as well as [æ], [a] < /a/ (Sara, 1974:34-5). This is, in essence, what Corré posits for Hebrew.

between *səgôl* and *pátaḥ* is entirely lacking in many Babylonian-pointed manuscripts.[5] Nor does any /e/ : *səgôl* : /a/ contrast turn up in earlier dialects, such as that of Origen's third-century Secunda.[6] Of course, *səgôl* was not a phoneme in Proto-Semitic, either — which is widely recognized to have had only */i/, */a/, and */u/. So if we need a systematic *səgôl* phoneme to handle segolates, we need it for only a few forms that arose relatively late in the transmission process.

In summation, then, if distributions in the biblical text point to a distinctive *səgôl* phoneme, they do so only in marginal ways, within historically late layers of the tradition. More importantly, though, any traces of its phonemicity in the surface structure can be explained (at least in structuralist and generative models) by adding a few morphophonemic or lexically conditioned rules (e.g., tagging *lêḥem* as a simple exception to the general rule).

## 4 Distribution vs. Perception

If biblical Hebrew *səgôl* was not a phoneme originally, and is at best only marginally so in the Tiberian Hebrew corpus, then why did the medieval Tiberian Masoretes introduce it so aggressively into their writing system? Formal linguists assure us that sub-phonemic variations (like the nasalization and lengthening of /æ/ discussed in section

---

5. The simple Babylonian system lacks *səgôl*, using *pátaḥ* instead. Manuscripts that use *səgôl* often restrict it to specific environments, such as closed syllables and *ḥāṭēp*-like positions. Sometimes *səgôl* alternates with *ḥāṭēp-pátaḥ* in unpredictable ways. Some apparently heard three vowel grades, [e], [ɛ], and [a]. Others heard only [e] and [a] — reinterpreting the *səgôl* sign as quantitative, or as morphologically determined. Similar variations exist in Palestinian-pointed MSS (Revell, 1970:102-3).

6. The Secunda uses *epsilon* and *alpha* to represent third-century CE Hebrew /e/, /a/, and /aː/ (Janssens, 1982: §25). *Epsilon* also represents /ɛː/. We know /ɛː/ existed because *-{i,a}yu# becomes Secundal *epsilon*, never *alpha*. *Epsilon* in this case indicates quality, not length (cf. the LXX, which transcribes this vowel as *eta*). Unlike Tiberian *səgôl*, /ɛː/ was intrinsically long, and restricted to word-final position.

2) usually go unnoticed, and so tend not to wend their way into writing systems evolved by native speakers of a language (see Sapir, 1949). Also, marginal phonemes like the /ts/ in the loan-word *tse-tse fly*, although often represented one way or another, generally do not bring about any massive reworkings of the orthography. Why is it, then, that the Masoretes introduced a distinct grapheme to represent *səgôl* — a vowel that is, in virtually every instance, just a reflex of the phonemes /e/ and /a/?

Although previous linguistically aware expositions have tended to explain such anomalies in the Tiberian system as due to its generally low-level phonetic character,[7] such an approach is misguided. The orthography is fully phonemic, in that it accurately represents the phonological perceptions of the Masoretes. Note, however, that those perceptions did not come about through exposure to native Hebrew speakers. From the laments of the medieval grammarians, it is obvious that Hebrew had long before died out as a vernacular language (Saenz-Badillos, 1993:205), probably even as early as 200 CE (Rabin, 1970:324).[8] Masoretic perceptions must have come, therefore, through cognitive mechanisms developed in conjunction with other languages. Given that they derive from other languages, and that they do not necessarily mirror the perceptions of the old Hebrew speech community, it should come as no surprise that these perceptions do not always reflect the intrinsic structure of the Hebrew preserved in the Tiberian Text.

## 5   Perception and the Phoneme

Let me put this all in less abstract terms. If we were to gather a bunch of Italians together and have them read some classical Latin out loud,

---

7. Enos (1992:47) calls the Masoretic analysis of Hebrew "an arbitrary mixture of levels." Wernberg-Møller (1974:124) labels the Masoretes "early phoneticians." Ornan (1964:111) calls the Tiberian orthography "phonetic."

8. Chomsky's fervent belief that Hebrew never died out (Chomsky, 1957:207-8) rests on false premises about the character of non-vernacular languages. Cf. early modern Latin (Benner and Tengström, 1977:64-85).

they would sound, to us, like Italians. Similarly, if we had a bunch of Israelis read passages from the Talmud, they would sound to us like Israelis. Likewise, if we had a bunch of Amharic speakers from Ethiopia read Ge'ez to us, they would end up sounding pretty much like Amharic speakers. Why? Because it is hard enough to shed one's "accent" when learning a living language. It is well nigh impossible to shed it when learning a *dead* one. Lacking native speakers to correct and compare oneself against, one's pronunciation habits inevitably gravitate toward some contemporary vernacular.

It really does not matter if, as in the Masoretic case, there is a strong and continuous stream of tradition. We know that even living speech communities with rigorous pronunciation standards change overtime. Especially on the lowest phonological levels, such changes are not even conscious. At every stage in a language's development, then, there is always a certain amount of vacillation and flux — regardless of whether speakers know it is happening, and regardless of whether the language in question is a living or a dead one. If anything, the degree of change is greater in the case of dead languages, since, at any given stage, ever-present forces of internal change will always be compounded by external pressures from living languages (Eldar, 1990:52).[9]

What is crucial here for us is that pronunciation and perception go hand-in-hand. In many dialects of American English, for example, the vowels /a/, /ɒ/, and /ɔ/ have coalesced. As a result, speakers of these dialects no longer perceive the difference between *cot* and *caught*, or *balm* and *bomb* — even when these words are pronounced by speakers who have all three vowels. Take also, for example, the case of N. American dialects that possess both /aɪ/ (representing the vowel in *bide*) and /ʌɪ/ (representing the vowel in *bite*). Speakers of such dialects hear a distinction where most of us hear only /aɪ/. This can lead to some interesting situations. Imagine, for example, a school

---

9. That Jewish Aramaic speakers might have preserved archaic quirks of their former Hebrew vernacular is not relevant here, because Tiberian *səgôl*, as such, was not an archaic Hebrew phoneme (cf. Corré, 1967:64).

teacher without /ʌɪ/ drilling students on the difference between "long" (i.e., tense) and "short" (i.e., lax) vowels. Students who heard the difference between /aɪ/ and /ʌɪ/ might well label the *i* in *writer* as a "short" /ʌɪ/ vowel. For the teacher, however, this would be incorrect. For him or her, *writer* would have the same ("long") vowel as *rider* and *slider*. The result would be hopeless confusion, as I myself can attest — this precise scenario having been played out in my son's grade-school classroom!

Though some would imbue the Masoretes with superhuman powers, their situation was really no different than my son's. The Masoretes possessed a perceptual distinction (in this instance, between /a/, /ɛ/ and /e/) that former Hebrew speakers lacked. And as a result, although the reading tradition shows almost no evidence of a distinctive *səgôl* phoneme, the Masoretes still wrote one, and did so with alacrity. What the Masoretes wrote, then, depended on what they perceived, and what they perceived arose, not from scientific analysis of the corpus, or from necromantic interactions with long-dead Hebrew speakers. Rather, it evolved from actual experience, i.e., from the languages they heard and used in their daily lives. Presumably these languages included several Aramaic dialects[10] and perhaps some Arabic ones as well. Of course, it really does not matter what languages they were speaking. What matters is simply that these languages, whatever they were, were not Hebrew.

We see modern analogues to the Masoretes' situation whenever speakers of one language try to learn another. Take, for example, the case of an English speaker who hears Japanese [l] and [r] as distinct, or the case of a German speaker who hears the [æː] in English *bad* as a true long */æː/ vowel (cf. the [æ] in *bat*). Such people often pronounce these sounds in exactly the same way as native speakers of the language. Where they diverge from native speakers is in how they perceive what they are doing. The English speaker may believe he is pronouncing two Japanese phonemes, /l/ and /r/, rather than two

---

10. Nestorian Syriac has *e*, *ɛ* and *a* signs. Jacobite texts have only one mid vowel sign, *e/ɛ*, though they sometimes import Nestorian *e* to get two such signs.

allophones of a single phoneme. Likewise, the German speaker may think he is pronouncing a true long English vowel, /æː/, rather than an allophone of the vowel /æ/ for which length is merely secondary. Significantly, if these non-native speakers were to develop systems for transcribing the sounds they heard, they would come up with systems that reflected their perceptions, rather than the inherent distributions of the sounds in their acquired language (Crowley, 1992:76 and n.1).

Though there were no native speakers to learn from, the Masoretes' situation was similar to those of our hypothetical English and German speakers. They knew a Hebrew reading tradition in which [ɛ] existed as an allophone of either /a/ or /e/. Yet their linguistic processing mechanisms told them that [ɛ] was its own phoneme, /ɛ/. Hence they transcribed [ɛ] using a distinct grapheme, *səgôl* — in effect violating the intrinsic structure of the language they were representing.

Interestingly, if the Masoretes had dropped, rather than added a vowel, information would have been lost. We observe precisely this sort of information loss in the Palestinian-pointed texts that show no distinction between *qāmeṣ* and *pátaḥ*, and therefore betray novel and/or confused patterns in the orthography of low vowels. In the case of Tiberian *səgôl*, though, information was not lost. Rather, it was merely reclassified.

Does all of this mean that Paul Kahle was right that the Masoretes were analysts, i.e., prescriptive trend setters? By no means. Much of what goes on phonologically in normal human speech falls well below the threshold of consciousness. This was the case for the Masoretes, who simply passed on what they learned as accurately as their cognitive mechanisms would allow. So, in fact, I am genuinely not attempting to resurrect the old, Kahle-esque view that the medieval reading traditions reflect extensive conscious grammatical, textual, or (as in this case) phonological analysis. Nor am I trying to impugn the continuity and basic integrity of the Masoretic transmission process. All I am claiming is that Masoretic linguistic behavior follows the same basic patterns as all human linguistic behavior. The Tiberian Masoretes wrote down *səgôl* for the simple reason that their living linguistic experiences led them to perceive that sound as distinct (so also Corré, 1967:60-62).

## 6 Wider Applications

The notion of linguistic perceptions as carrying over from living to dead languages naturally has application to phenomena other than *səgôl*. Consistent graphic differentiation between the stop and fricative pronunciations of the *bgdkpt* letters in Tiberian Hebrew, for example, probably has nothing to do with superficial or hypothetical contrasts such as *šṭe[h]* 'drink' : *šte[y]* 'two of', and *ʔalp̄e[y]* 'thousands of' : *\*ʔalpe[y]* 'two thousand of'. It is far more likely that orthographic differentiation between stops and their corresponding fricatives reflects perceptual distinctions gained by exposure to Arabic and/or Aramaic substrata, where these contrasts were more critical. For example, imagine mistaking /t/ for /θ/ in Arabic, or trying to pronounce Arabic /f/ as Aramaic [p] (Arabs might have mistaken [p] for /b/). Note also that Hellenistic Greek had both /p/ and /ɸ/ (< older /pʰ/) phonemes.

Solution of such intra- and cross-dialectal difficulties would have provided ample opportunity for the Tiberian scholars to acquire perceptual distinctions between stop and fricative pronunciations of the *bgdkpt* letters — and this, despite huge complications that these distinctions end up adding to lexical representations (at least in more recent generative models), and thus to the overall size of the Tiberian Hebrew grammar.

Incidentally, in claiming a language-external motivation for the Masoretes' handling of *dāḡēš*, I am not so much denying J. Malone's (1975) hypothesis that descriptivists' autonomous phonemes best explain this aspect of the orthography as I am offering another — more natural — explanation for the phenomenon. We know that the Masoretes spoke non-Hebrew vernaculars. So analysis of how they handled the Hebrew reading tradition is bound to reveal a few clashes between their perceptions and the text. Masoretic use of the *dāḡēš* where systematic analysis tells us it was not strictly required is a perfect example of such a clash. It reflects precisely the sort of vernacular carry-over we expect to find whenever a community tries to preserve a dead language.

## 7  Conclusion

Rather than sift through countless pieces of raw linguistic data, rather, in efforts to prove this or that thesis about *səgôl*'s phonemic status, this study has, focused on whether such standard analytical methods are even appropriate in this case. The reality is that one's answer to the question, "Is Tiberian Hebrew *səgôl* a phoneme?" depends far more on one's predisposition toward the Tiberian Text than on anything in the text itself. One's answer is "yes" to the extent that one thinks of that text as recording the perceptions of scholars who had never met a native Hebrew speaker. One's answer is "no", however, to the extent that one thinks of it historically, as a kind of storehouse of information about how Hebrew was spoken back when it was still a living language. One's answer, finally, is "maybe" to the extent that one thinks of the it distributionally, as providing us with raw data about an old liturgical reading dialect. Whether or not one designates *səgôl* a phoneme in this last instance is more a matter of theoretical taste than of actual data. If, for example, one posits lexical *səgôl* for *léḥɛm*, then the answer is probably "yes". Otherwise it would tend towards "no".

Even if one admits *səgôl* as a marginal phoneme, however, one is still left with a quandary: Why were the Masoretes so exacting about representing it? This quandary, as I have shown above, disappears the moment we remember that the Masoretes lived hundreds of years after the last native Hebrew speaker drew his or her last breath. The Masoretes' phonological perceptions, therefore, do not reflect Hebrew speech patterns. Rather, they reflect the patterns characteristic of other languages — languages that the Masoretes heard in everyday life; languages that presumably possessed phonemes Hebrew lacked; languages that led the Masoretes to transcribe Hebrew in a way that did not jibe with its intrinsic phonological structure.

Although solving the problem of *səgôl*'s phonemicity might seem a purely theoretical endeavor, it has certain practical ramifications that are well worth consideration. For one thing, *səgôl*'s anomalous presence in the Tiberian writing system reminds us that the Masoretes were not superhuman phoneticians. They were intelligent, devoted, and extraordinarily thorough scholars. But they were, after all, just people like us — subject to the same cognitive limitations that the rest of us are subject to.

Perhaps the most important ramification of this inquiry into *səgôl*'s phonemic status, however, is that it underscores an essential methodological point, namely that any effort at dealing with Tiberian Hebrew phonology must inevitably come to terms with the plain fact that Tiberian Hebrew is not a natural language. In reality, Tiberian Hebrew *per se* consists of a closed, chanted corpus that has passed through the filter of many non-native speakers' misperceptions. Sadly, linguists and philologists today typically treat the Tiberian Text with great naiveté — as if it were phoneticians' field notes, and could be treated like a transcript of living speech. Although it is frequently analytically advantageous to work under this fallacy, one must never forget that it is, in fact, a fallacy, and that the real situation presents far too many complications for any currently available formal linguistic framework to deal fully and effectively with it.

168 / *Richard L. Goerwitz*

## References

Benner, M. and E. Tengström. 1977.
*On the Interpretation of Learned Neo-Latin.* (Studia Graeca et Latina Gothoburgensia 39), Göteborg: Acta Universitatis Gothoburgensis.

Bloomfield, L. c. 1933.
*Language.* New York: H. Holt.

Cantineau, J. 1950.
Essai d'une phonologie de l'hébreu biblique. *Bulletin de la Société Linguistique de Paris,* 46:82-122.

Chomsky, N. and M. Halle. 1968.
*The Sound Pattern of English.* New York: Harper and Row.

Chomsky, W. 1957.
*Hebrew: The Eternal Language.* Gitelson Library. Philadelphia: Jewish Publication Society of America.

Corré, A. D. 1967.
Phonemic Problems in the Masora. In *Essays Presented to Chief Rabbi Israel Brodie on the Occasion of his Seventieth Birthday,* edd. H. J. Zimmels, J. Rabbinowitz, and I. Finestein, pp. 59-66. (Jew's College Publications, New Series 3). London: Soncino Press.

Crowley, T. 1992.
*An Introduction to Historical Linguistics.* Auckland: Oxford University Press.

Eldar, I. 1990.
Hebrew Reading Traditions of the Jewish Communities. In *VIII International Congress of the International Organization for Masoretic Studies* (Masoretic Studies 6), ed. E. J. Revell, pp. 45-64. Atlanta: Scholars Press.

Enos, G. 1992.
Phonological Considerations in the Study of Hebrew Phonetics: An Introductory Discussion. In *Linguistics and Biblical Hebrew,* ed. W. R. Bodine, pp. 41-47. Winona Lake, Indiana: Eisenbrauns.

Halle, M. 1964.
On the Bases of Phonology. In *The Structure of Language,* edd. J. A. Fodor and J. J. Katz, pp. 324-333. Englewood Ciffs: Prentice Hall.

Jakobson, R. C. 1962.
Observations sur le classement phonologique des consonnes. In *Selected Writings,* vol. 1. s-Gravenhage: Mouton. (Originally published in the Proceedings of the Third International Congress of Phonetic Sciences. Ghent, 1939).

Jakobson, R. C., G. M. Fant and M. Halle. 1967.
*Preliminaries to Speech Analysis; the Distinctive Features and their Correlates.*
Cambridge, Massachusetts: MIT Press.

Janssens, G. 1982.
*Studies in Hebrew Historical Linguistics Based on Origen's Secunda.* (Orientalia Gandensia 9). Leuven: Uitgeverij Peeters.

Johnson, R. M. Jr., and R. L. Goerwitz. 1995.
A Simple, Practical System for Transliterating Tiberian Hebrew Vowels. Forthcoming in *Hebrew Studies* 36:13-24.

Malone, J. L. 1975.
*Systematic vs. Autonomous Phonemics and the Hebrew Grapheme Dagesh.* (Monographic Journals of the Near East. Afroasiatic Linguistics, vol. 2[7]). Malibu, California: Undena Publications. (Part of the Proceedings of the First North-American Conference on Semitic Linguistics, Santa Barbara, California, March 24-25, 1973.)

Mohanan, K. P. 1986.
*The Theory of Lexical Phonology.* (Studies in Natural Language and Linguistic Theory 6). Dordrecht, Boston: D. Reidel. Distributed in the U.S.A. and Canada by Kluwer Academic (Norwell, MA).

Ornan, U. 1964.
The Tiberian Vocalization System and the Principles of Linguistics. *Journal of Jewish Studies* 15:109-123.

Rabin, C. 1970.
Hebrew. *Current Trends in Linguistics*, vol. 6, pp. 304-346. The Hague: Mouton.

Revell, E. J. 1970.
*Hebrew Texts with Palestinian Vocalization.* (Near and Middle East Series 7). Toronto: University of Toronto Press.

Revell, E. J. 1976.
Bibilical Punctuation and Chant in the Second Temple Period. *Journal for the Study of Judaism* 7:181-198.

Revell, E. J. 1985.
The Vowelling of 'i Type' Segolates in Tiberian Hebrew. *Journal of Near Eastern Studies* 44:319-328.

Saenz-Badillos, A. 1993.
*A History of the Hebrew Language.* Translated by J. Elwolde. Cambridge: Cambridge University Press.

170 / *Richard L. Goerwitz*

Sapir, E. 1949.
*Selected Writings in Language, Culture, and Personality.* Ed. D. G. Mandelbaum. Berkeley: University of California Press.

Sara, S. L. 1974.
*A Description of Modern Chaldaean.* (Janua Linguarum, Series Practica, 213). The Hague and Paris: Mouton.

Saussure, F. de 1974.
*Course in General Linguistics* (revised ed.). Edd. C. Bally, A. Sechehaye, and A. Reidlinger. Translated by W. Baskin. London: Fontana.

Trubetzköy, N. S. 1969.
*Principles of Phonology.* Translated by C. A. M. Baltaxe. Berkeley: University of California Press.

Wernberg-Møller, P. 1974.
Aspects of Masoretic Vocalization. In *1972 and 1973 Proceedings, IOMS* (Masoretic Studies 1), ed. H. M. Orlinsky, pp. 121-130. Missoula, Montana: Scholars Press.

**Acknowledgments**
This paper has benefitted, in particular, from comments offered by Henry Churchyard, Peter Daniels, and Robert Hoberman. I am also indebted to various respondents present at the 1994 (Chicago) Society of Biblical Literature meetings. Such respondents include Saul Levin, Gary Rendsburg, and Douglas Gropp. Finally, I would like to thank my good friend, Alan Corré, who called his 1967 article to my attention after this one was nearly complete, prompting me to make substantial changes to this final version.

Lightning Source UK Ltd.
Milton Keynes UK
UKHW041033051118
331799UK00001B/135/P